BEAT THE CUTS

How to improve **public services** and easily cut costs

BEAT
THE CUTS

How to improve
public services
and easily cut costs

ROB WORTH

www.ecademy-press.com

Beat the Cuts

First published in 2011 by;

Ecademy Press

48 St Vincent Drive, St Albans, Herts, AL1 5SJ

info@ecademy-press.com

www.ecademy-press.com

Set in Warnock and Antique Olive by Karen Gladwell

Cover artwork and illustrations by Michael Inns

Printed on acid-free paper from managed forests. This book is printed on demand, so no copies will be remaindered or pulped.

ISBN 978-1-907722-72-1

Contents

Introduction

The government is cutting public sector budgets. We have already seen cuts to local services such as libraries, Sure Start centres and youth work to name a few. In addition, in the NHS some areas have cancelled certain types of treatments and waiting lists have been getting longer.

We can continue the easy, obvious path, which is to cut yet more services and further cut the resources for the services that remain. We can follow this with outsourcing and putting delivery in manufacturing-like call centres and shared service facilities.

If we continue to do this, public services will be decimated. We might make short-term cuts in costs, but in the long term, costs in the remaining, under-resourced services will bounce back. Costs will spring back because doing work badly is more expensive due to the cost of the rework needed to rectify the errors. In addition there is the cost of dealing with all the calls, letters, emails and visits from members of the public complaining that their service is bad and is taking too long.

We don't have to do it that way. We can "Beat the Cuts". We can save services and cut costs. The way to do it is to improve services. Only then will costs come down.

Working with a government department on their annual returns process we found that less than 10% of their process steps added value and 50% of the calls into the call centre could be prevented by not making errors in processing and dealing with forms quicker.

It is quite common to have 50% wasteful demand and 90% waste in processes. So if we can cut 50% of the work and 90% of the work that is left, significant budget savings don't seem so hard.

We need to look beyond dealing with services as simply transactional and move past the simplification of always studying demand first. Public services are complex human systems and we need to identify principles and problem solving methods that deal with this complexity. We must rise above the noise of the latest improvement fads to provide long-lasting skills that endure and get results.

The best part is that you can realise results in weeks, not months or years. It is about a different way of looking at the work and not about big programmes and projects.

This book will show the public sector what to look at, what to ignore, and how to improve services and make savings so they can get the same amazing results as the government department.

Who should read this book?

This book is aimed at public sector workers from chief executives to the front line staff as well as councillors, politicians and anyone else who has an interest in the public sector delivering good services. We all need to know about the new roles in a different way of working. All our jobs will change. Staff doing the work will have the added responsibility of improving the work. Management who currently design the work will stop doing so and instead will take the role of supporting the staff. Upper management who currently issue orders that are supposed to cascade down the hierarchy will now take true responsibility for seeing the system as a whole and communicating that view to the rest of the organisation.

A note about naming

Throughout this book the public who use services will normally be referred to as the "customer" except when a specific service is referenced, e.g. tenant for housing repairs. I don't like the term customer, because it has the wrong connotations. I recommend that if you have a more relevant name for a customer in your service such as tenant, patient, passenger or similar then you should use it. Those names will mesh more closely with the reason for your service.

I will refer to three levels of organisational worker: staff, management and upper management. Staff are those who work at the front line. Upper management are the chief executives, members of the board and very senior staff. Management is everyone else in between.

Section 1

Fundamental Ideas

Chapter 1
Improving service cuts cost

The system is the structure,

the reason is the why,

what customers value is the measure,

but the work is the cause.

In these economically straitened times, the government is slashing services to cut the deficit to manageable levels. Whether or not you agree with the economic arguments that we need to cut now, the public sector needs a practical way to deal with these cuts. In the public sector we can watch as the government cuts services to save money or we can offer another way; a method that will not only save services but also deliver the required budgetary savings.

It is not merely that it is possible to maintain services while cutting budgets. It is actually that making improvements to services is the only reliable way to cut the costs of delivering services and hence offer the savings back to the taxpayer.

Cutting cost leads to worse service, which in turn leads to higher costs.

Improved service leads to lower costs.

Broken cost-service seesaw

Imagine cost and service on a seesaw. Cost is on one end and service on the other. The underlying assumption is that by pushing on one end of the seesaw we can predictably affect the other end. On the cost end, higher means greater costs, and on the service end, higher means better service.

The first instinct when cuts come along is to push down hard on the cost end of the seesaw, but this causes service to worsen as programmes are slashed and the resources left for the remaining work dwindle.

The worst of it is that as service worsens, costs will go back up – the seesaw will spring back up on the cost side. This is because with worse service you are dealing with massive extra wasteful contacts and broken processes because you have no resource to fix them. You start throwing money at backlog busting and hiring private sector companies to sort out the mess. Hence cost goes up.

Pushing down on cost causes service to get worse and soon costs will rise.

The alternative is that we lift the quality of services by creating processes to deliver customer value, design out wasteful contacts and remove waste. We see that as services get better, costs fall, and they fall further than we could have predicted from a cost/benefit study.

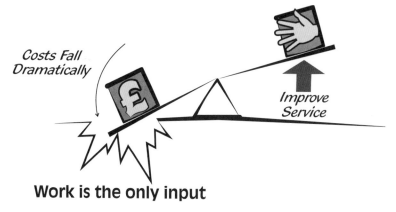

Work is the only input

It is not just budgets that benefit from this causal direction.

In his book *Obliquity*,* the economist John Kay argues that many of the things we seek – happiness, wealth, etc. – are not best approached directly but rather they need to be attacked from angles that are not at first obvious. Further, he argues that directly approaching certain problems will lead to the opposite of the desired effect. As Paul Simon wrote in his famous song, "The nearer your destination, / The more you're slip sliding away."

John Kay cites wealth as a good example. It brings to mind the characters that populate the BBC show *The Apprentice*, in which the

---

*Kay, John. *Obliquity: Why Our Goals Are Best Achieved Indirectly*, Profile Books (2010).

supposedly best-of-the-best vie for the chance to become the next apprentice to Alan Sugar. They are all tackling the problem directly and seem to spend their time fighting and stabbing each other in the back while trying to paint a veneer of working as a team. The best business people I know come at it from a totally oblique point of view. Their aim is to assist their fellow business people, to help others and to provide as much value to the market so customers will want to come back. True business people know we are all in this together.

Wealth is about helping others so together you can provide value. If you provide enough value, people will be happy to give you money in return.

In the public sector a very similar mechanism operates. If you provide the public with a good service then all the outcomes that currently people try to achieve directly will happen naturally.

The desired state

What we are aiming for is a situation where:

> **Every service provides maximum value to customers as quickly as possible, with no waste, delay or rework.**

If we can achieve this state then all the other desired things fall into place. There is no need to work on them directly.

Budget – With no waste, wasteful contacts, delay or rework there can't be a cheaper way of doing the work. Funding would be at a minimum for a given service.

Culture – The culture in such a service would be excellent. There is no way that you could construct such a way of working without somehow getting people to communicate well, work together and support each other. It is doing a good job that pulls people together, not the other way around.

Morale – This is similar to culture. Morale would be excellent in such a high achieving place, but you can't create morale out of thin air. No matter how chief executives try to convince us that we can think

6

or persuade our staff into having good morale, we can't. Improve the service, do well, and morale will get better and better.

Sickness and absenteeism – With interesting work, great teams to work in and compelling problems to solve, will people come into work or bunk off? Much work goes into directly trying to reduce these headaches, but only by creating a place of work that people actually want to come to will you reduce these problems. The bonus is that it doesn't cost extra and you can drop the absenteeism programme, which then saves even more money.

Creativity – Creativity is a function of time to think, exposure to new ideas and an opportunity to experiment in a safe environment. We are creating the time to think and the opportunity to express ideas in our HELP* sessions every day. HELP is also the opportunity to experiment with those ideas in a robust and supported way.

Engagement – People will be engaged in a situation where you have a great culture, where you are working to improve the way that you deliver important services and where they can see the higher purpose. No number of employee engagement programmes can create this. People decide for themselves whether they are engaged or not. Give them good work and the responsibility to make it better and they will engage themselves.

Good work costs less

Returning to the money side of things in more detail is important since it is this that we are reeling from in the public sector. Cuts are already being made to services that could have been saved if only work was being done more effectively.

There are several wastes in service when work is not done very well.

---

*The HELP cycle is explained in Chapter 6.

Waste of delay

The first reason delays cost money is that the delayed work must somehow be stored. For work on paper there will be the pigeonholes, archive boxes, in-trays and filing systems. Sometimes it is simply piled on the floor. Then there is the effort of getting that work in and out of these storage systems.

What causes delays? The root cause is a mismatch between demand and capacity. If the capacity is less than demand then work will pile up at some point and sit there until that process can catch up. If the capacity is not raised then there will be waiting lists and those waiting lists will grow.

More interesting is where the completed work coming out of the end of the process is emerging at the same rate as work is arriving. In this situation there is no reason for a backlog at all.

For example, suppose there are ten planning applications completed every day and ten planning applications arrive every day, if the process is designed properly there should be no reason why the work arriving should not start the process as soon as it arrives. However, it is common that there are waiting lists and backlogs that are neither shrinking or growing for all sorts of services including planning, surgical operations, childcare, getting a social worker appointed and many more.

The major causes of delay within a process are batching and sorting. There is the belief in economies due to scale. Scale is only applicable to work that is repeatable, so there is much effort in sorting work into similar batches and then working on those batches all at one time. For example, a dermatologist might see all his psoriasis patients one day in a psoriasis clinic and the following day run an eczema clinic. This means that new eczema patients have to wait until the relevant clinic comes around instead of just taking the next free, convenient appointment.

In a government department's Annual Return section there was much activity to do with batching and sorting forms into like piles. A pile of 20 forms would contain forms of the same colour, which meant they were from organisations of the same size and covered the same reporting year. E.g. a pile of 20 grape coloured forms would all be for organisations with income of less than £10k reporting for the 2009 cycle.

The problem is that when the forms were keyed in, they were picked off the batches one at a time. So what would be the difference between picking up a grape form followed by a puce form followed by a yellow form rather than picking 20 grape forms one after the other? None as it turned out. The batching and sorting was adding no value at all.

Delays also cause the public to chase progress. When a request takes longer than you think it will, you call up the service to find out what is going on. Taking this call and finding the status takes time and money and drags resource away from doing the core work. So if you can do the work in less time, you get fewer progress-chasing wasteful contacts, meaning you have more time to do the work even more quickly.

Waste of errors

Errors cause rework. That rework is a cost in effort and time. This causes delays. Worse, uncaught errors move along the process and cause errors and delay further downstream. The downstream errors are typically bigger and harder to fix than the original error.

As the saying goes, "A stitch in time saves nine."

It is estimated that it takes four times longer to fix an error than it does to complete the original task correctly the first time round. And the time taken to commit an error is the same as doing it right.

There is the concept of error proofing,* which means putting in place mechanisms that prevent erroneous acts by making them impossible to commit.

---

*Error proofing is also known as poka-yoke. This is a term from Japan and commonly used in Lean thinking

Think of putting your credit card in a payment machine. Who hasn't put it in with the chip on the wrong side or on top when it should be on the bottom? Now think of a SIM card in a mobile phone. Similar to a credit card, it is also a rectangle that needs to go the right way round and the right way up. However, a SIM card has a corner cut off it, meaning that in order to get the shape to match, you are forced to put it in the mobile phone the right way round.

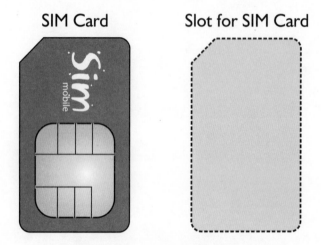

SIM Card   Slot for SIM Card

You can only put a **SIM Card** in the correct way round

Similar ideas prevent you proceeding to submit a web form until you have entered a validly formed email address.

Chapter 2

Customer provides the reason

An essential step in improving

a service is to state the

reason for it to exist.

Statement of the reason

The statement of the reason is a sentence describing what the service is here to do. This short statement will keep the staff and management on the straight and narrow when later judging whether process changes, new measures or alterations to service delivery are improving the service or worsening it.

The reason is derived from customer value.

It is not important that the statement of the reason should be perfect, just that it should be useful and meaningful at the time of use.

As the process of studying the work goes on, the statement of the reason will be revisited and revised to better fit understanding as it evolves.

The reason will ensure that we are doing the right thing. To paraphrase Russell Ackoff, it is better to do the right thing wrong than to do the wrong thing brilliantly.

Many organisations don't have any expression of the reason. The staff, managers and customers of these organisations have no real idea what they are ultimately aiming for. They have no image to compare themselves, their actions or decisions to.

The reason why we are here

The reason is a simply stated, common idea of the point of the organisation: the reason why we are here. We need to compare ourselves and what we do against something meaningful and useful. The statement of the reason is it. As we go about our business, day by day, we can think about the reason for the organisation, ponder our place in it and judge whether we are advancing that aim or hindering it. In this context, not moving forward is a hindrance in the world today.

When it comes to the reason, clarity is king. Though clarity is not very common.

Don't have long mission and values

Most organisations that do have a statement fall for the "mission and values" trap. They send top management off on an expensive off-site trip where they examine evidence from equally expensive focus group sessions and customer surveys. The highly experienced executives put in their own two penneth and take two days to come up with paragraphs of vague, meaningless waffle.

Here is an example from the side of a coffee mug from a north London borough council:

Our Vision

To measurably improve the quality of life for the people of [the borough] by tackling some of our biggest problems and making it a borough we can all be proud of.

It is a typical example of vagueness, compromise and a need to try and cover all the bases.

The problem with overly lofty mission and value statements is that though they can be very heart-warming to upper management, often front line staff will not identify with them. One of the uses of the reason is to give a common understanding of why we are here. Airy-fairy, head-in-the-clouds professions of brotherly and sisterly love to the world will simply turn off the public and the people who do the work.

The statement of the reason needs to keep its feet on the ground so that everyone can see its relevance.

An example of a good, concise statement of a reason is that of the Los Angeles Police Department:

To Protect and Serve.

This simple phrase helps residents of Los Angeles understand the point of the LAPD. The officers on duty have a succinct measure of whether they are doing the job they are supposed to do as they reflect on that motto.

The stated reason should be focused, obvious and clear. It must not be woolly or trying to achieve things that are out of the control of the organisation.

Something the customer would agree with

It should state the "reason we are here". It should be something that a customer would immediately agree with. It should be as if the customer had defined the reason.

For example, the reason for the refuse service in a local authority is not anything to do with making "a borough we can be proud of". If you were to ask householders and business owners what the point of the service was, they would reply something like, "To collect my rubbish."

So a good possible reason for a refuse service might be:

Collect and dispose of rubbish and recycling.

> ### For the Highways Department it could be:
>
> ## *Keep the roads in good repair.*

These are short, obvious, clear statements that the public would agree with and understand.

Keep it short

As a guide on length, one sentence is usually enough and two is plenty. If you are tempted into two or more sentences or sentences with several clauses and commas, then you are probably straying into catchall territory while saying nothing.

Take away until nothing else can be cut. Cut, cut and cut again until you make the point, short and sweet.

Some more examples:

> ### An Accident and Emergency department:
>
> ## *To assess and treat emergency medical needs.*

> ### Adult social care:
>
> ## *To meet the housing and medical needs of the elderly.*

Exercise:

Try and think of a succinct statement of a reason for the following examples:

1. **The ambulance service**

2. **Social services**

3. **Educational welfare officers**

Chapter 3

Appreciation for a system

The biggest mistake is to see an organisation as a collection of parts and then work to improve the parts individually.

A system is a collection of interconnected parts. It is how well the parts work together, not how well the parts function individually, that is the major factor that governs the overall performance of the system.

Russell Ackoff gives the analogy of a car. Think of an ordinary saloon car. It works very well. It is not the fastest, the best handling or the coolest car, but it does the job of getting the driver and passengers from A to B. What if we tried to optimise the engine? We could take an engine from a Formula One racing car and try to put it in our ordinary saloon. Even if we could make it fit we would have to start making alterations to the transmission and other parts to get it to run properly. Now we have an ordinary car with a massively powerful engine. If we try to run that engine at even half speed we will probably shake the car to bits, so we will need to strengthen the chassis. But now the suspension is groaning under the strain and we can't corner properly at the speeds that our new engine can take us. So the workaday shocks are replaced. We can see that we will have to change almost everything about the car to cope with the new Formula One engine. The resulting car will probably be a terrible compromise and it probably won't run very well.

Both Formula One racing cars and regular saloon cars work well because they are designed as a system with the way that the parts work together taking higher precedence than each individual part.

Analysis and synthesis

The skill of the scientist and the engineer is the ability to take things apart, understand the parts, optimise them and put them back together. This is analysis.

Apart from all the knowledge that gets stuffed into our heads, analysis is the main skill that we learn at school and university. Think of all the dissections of frogs, deconstructing Hemingway and Shakespeare, understanding bodies in motion and identifying the different types of rocks in a cliff side. Every time we seek to break down, examine parts, classify and name we are engaging in analysis.

Management is seen very much as an analytical discipline. Think of the way MBAs are taught in parts: economics, marketing, sales, people management, finance, and operations. It is no wonder that asset stripping is so popular and that the securitisation of assets to be split into separate products to be sold on was so prevalent up to the recent financial crisis.

We manage our organisations with analysis. Now that cuts are being asked for, the method that is most common is to look at the list of departments and services and to ask which can we axe, which can we outsource and of the rest, how can we make them more efficient?

The much less common skill is to be able to put things together in a harmonious way. Synthesis is the construction of a whole to achieve a purpose where the parts are subservient to that whole, just like in the example of the saloon car and the Formula One car. There are disciplines like ecology – and in physics there is the search for the Grand Unified Theory – that use more synthesis than analysis. Design is also a process of synthesis.

A house is a system. All the rooms and its layout should work in harmony to make the house a pleasant place in which to live. An architect may have to take space from a bedroom to make a bathroom that is suitable for the number of people expected to live in a house of that size. Similar considerations have to be made with the size and layout of the kitchen, dining room and living room. These might be omitted or combined depending on the family that the house is designed for.

A laptop computer is another excellent example. The compromise of power, weight and size means that the specification of the whole is set at the beginning. The parts – screen, hard drive, processor, DVD drive, etc. – are synthesised together to make a well-functioning machine.

We should seek the harmony of synthesis when designing services and service delivery. The reason defines the system and the design should start from there. Seek to satisfy the customer and optimise the whole.

Performance of a system

A system is perfectly designed to do what it does.

This means that if we want a system to do something different we need to change the system. We shall see later in the book that management instinct is often to work on the people, expecting that if they do better, then the system will do better. It is more effective to work on the system. As we redesign the work to achieve the reason so the performance of the people will improve as a consequence. The logic does not follow the other way around.

A simple system that demonstrates this is a 4-by-100-metre relay team. Of course if the individuals run faster, the team will do better. In fact, it is the teams that have the smoothest handovers that do better overall. The point of optimisation is to work on the baton exchange. It is the interaction between the parts that is the biggest opportunity to improve the team's performance as a whole.

Child protection is an even more complicated system where social workers, police, educational welfare officers, doctors and psychologists have to work together to achieve the best outcome for the children and their families. You may have the most efficient social workers, but if they are not passing relevant, timely information to the other professionals then the outcomes for the children in their care are much worse than they would be if everyone talked together.

There is much talk of joined up thinking and working, but this is still normally very localised. The view of the system as a whole is very rarely taken.

Public services are systems

When we come to look at public services we need to think in terms of systems. Optimisation of the parts is not as important as optimising the whole. The aim of optimising the whole is to become better at achieving the reason.

When we act on one part of a public sector organisation, we need to ask whether we are optimising the whole or just the part. Removing the taking of calls to a central call centre for a local authority may seem like it is making call taking cheaper. If the call centre causes the public to be more disconnected from those who do the work and this causes more calls to the call centre to rectify mistakes and chase progress, then this local optimisation has worsened the service to the public by the authority as a whole.

We can step out further and realise that public services are part of a bigger system. Society is made up of geography, economics, business, history, art and culture. How services fit together to serve society is important. It is the function of government to ensure that public services fit into the bigger system to promote society as a whole.

Total Place

Total Place was an idea that budgets should be transferable in an area across very separate services. The NHS and adult social care have many duplications and dependencies in most areas. The idea was, for example, that if a hospital trust was getting a high demand from falls by elderly people then budget could be diverted to the social care pot of the local authority to assist people to alter their homes to make them less prone to falls. They might have handrails fitted and new carpets that were less likely to trip them. I visited one area where they provided new slippers every six months because old slippers were an identified fall risk.

Total Place had its direction right, but in many of the pilots it was simply a money counting exercise. If some similar idea could be made to work where the whole system in an area could be made to work together, it would produce amazing results. Until it is understood that chasing the money will actually lead to greater cost, this will not work.

Chapter 4

Understanding variation

We all have an intuitive understanding of variation.

If we roll a dice ten times we would be very surprised if it came up six every time. Even if we tried our hardest to replicate the way we held the dice, to get the flick of the wrist exactly as before and the time of letting fly identical, we know that there will be slight variations in how we do it. That is not to mention that the dice will hit the table at a slightly different point, at a different speed, etc. As a consequence the number on the top face of a dice will vary as we throw it. If it didn't, gambling and board games would be very boring indeed.

It is also instructive to note that the dice varies predictably. It is not very likely that on a flat table the dice will end up on one of its points. It is not impossible, just very unlikely. This issue of variation within predictable limits is important and one we will revisit later.

A journey to work

Let's take a more day-to-day example. Imagine that you drive to work every day and that it takes 30 minutes to get there. Does it take exactly 30 minutes every day? Of course not. Some days it is sunny and on others it rains. Some days you hit the traffic lights just right and sometimes you have to wait. Some days are school holidays and some not. But it takes about 30 minutes, sometimes 25, sometimes 35.

However, if it were to take 90 minutes one day then something must have gone drastically wrong. Perhaps a fallen tree blocked your normal route or you had a puncture and had to change a tyre.

We make a distinction between the usual causes of variation like the weather, the traffic light timings and school holidays as being common causes. The fallen tree and the puncture are called special causes.

In the journey to work we have defined the special causes because we know them when we see them. The trick is to be able to look at a set of data and be able to point to a special cause simply because of the deviation from the normal variation.

Let's look at the time taken to travel to work over 20 days:

28, 33, 29, 30, 31, 31, 27, 35, 29, 31, 30, 32, 33, 28, 31, 30, 28, 27, 30, 32

We can see that they are all around 30 minutes; some are exactly 30 minutes, but most are a little longer or a little shorter.

Here is the same data on a chart with the average of 30.3 minutes added.

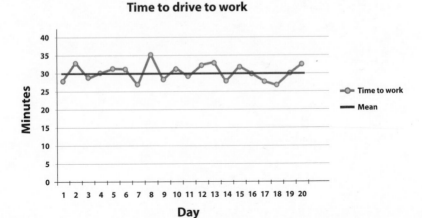

Time to drive to work

This data looks quite random. It is jumping up and down, but we know intuitively that it is about 30 minutes to get to work and the ups and downs are caused by the common causes like the weather and traffic lights. We know it is predictable since we need to leave slightly more than 30 minutes to get to work, and we don't worry about the lightning strikes and earthquakes since they don't figure too often in our morning routine.

What we need is a solid repeatable way to see if this data, and hence any data, is predictable or not.

The method to use is called Statistical Process Control (SPC).

SPC is a way of calculating limits* from a run of data such that if the data points all fall within the limits then the data is predictable, i.e. it is a working assumption that the next time this process is followed the result will also land between the limits. So let us apply this to our morning drive data.

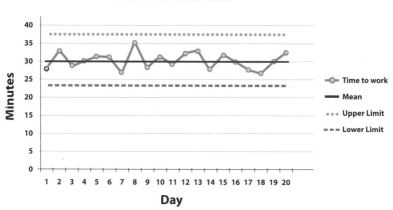

This is the SPC chart of our drive to work with the upper limit calculated to be 37.5 minutes and the lower limit is 23.0 minutes.

---

*The limits are approximately three standard deviations from the mean. This is just a guide since the method is designed to deal with any distribution of data, not just that which conforms to a normal curve. Suffice it to say that the limits show what is normal variation and what is not. The non-statistician simply needs to know that it is a useful method.

We can see that all the points fall within the limits, so we can predict with confidence that our next journey time will fall somewhere between 23.0 and 37.5 minutes.

If the next day it took 50 minutes to get to work, then we can say that something special happened and it needs to be investigated.

Let us take a similar data set that is not predictable.

Time to drive to work

We can see that event 8 has a special cause that falls above the upper limit and event 16 a low value under the calculated lower limit. These are special causes.

This data set is not predictable, and we cannot with any confidence predict what the journey time tomorrow might be.

This is important since we can now apply this technique to other areas.

Processing claims

Take for example the number of claims processed by a member of staff every day. His manager sees that he does 28 one day then 33 the next. The manager will be very happy. But then he does 29. What is happening? He is slipping. 30, 31, 31 follow, which are okay, but where did the 33 go? Surely he is capable of that every day? He did it once, why not again? Next day he processes 27 forms. Oh dear. Better have a word...

The sharp-eyed reader will have spotted that the sequence of claims completed is the same as the times taken to get to work in the first example. We are comfortable with the idea that the time taken to drive to work will vary, so why do we frequently feel the need to give reasons for the common cause fluctuations in performance measures at work? Do we not see managers hunkered over just these types of figures with minions tasked to write reports explaining every single up and down?

If we use SPC we can see that the member of staff will predictably handle between 23 and 38 forms every day. So if he does 24 or 37 tomorrow then there is nothing special going on, it is just down to common cause in the system and his manager shouldn't take any notice.

If, however, the claims processing looks like our unpredictable chart with the 70 and the 4 values in the series, they are outside the limits and the specific special causes should be identified and eliminated until we can again say that the performance is predictable.

Economy of action

This technique and the analysis above are all about whether, when and what type of action should be taken.

We are trying to avoid two errors:

1. Treating common cause variation as special

2. Treating special cause variation as common

In the first error we are reacting to every little up and down that is actually variation due to the system. We can only affect this variation by working on the system as a whole. Trying to find the specific cause of this variation is both fruitless and wasteful.

Treating special causes as common means we are missing important signals that something unique is going on. Not hunting these down will mean opening your system up to chaos. You can't begin to work on the common cause variation by working on the system until the special causes have been removed, so you have to take note.

If SPC shows special causes, you need to work on those first to remove them and make the process predictable. Once the process is stable you can work on the system to reduce the common cause variation (narrow the limits) and move the average in the right direction. In the case of the journey to work it would be nice to have a lower average, and in the case of processing claims every day, his manager would want a higher average.[*]

---

[*] Claims per day is a measure of busyness and therefore should not be optimised, but instead replaced with a measure of purpose.

Chapter 5

Flow and pull

The aim is work that moves
smoothly with value being
constantly added.

Follow the process

After we begin to understand our system and the value to the customer, we can examine the processes that deliver the value.

Customers experience value end to end. They don't understand the different departmental silos that are common in organisations, nor should they have to. It is very frustrating to have people in every department denying knowledge of a problem and it being continuously passed from department to department with nobody able to take ownership of the whole problem. Customers ask themselves, "Why don't they just talk to each other?"

It has been suggested that organisations reorganise themselves along value streams and that idea has merit. A full argument of the pros and cons of that is beyond the scope of this book, but suffice it to say that a reorientation along the flow of value would do organisations the power of good. We must see work the way our customers see it, and they don't see departmental walls on organisation charts.

Flow

Taiichi Ohno's core principle at Toyota was to get value to the customer as quickly as possible. This is a good place to start.

Principles of flow

1. **Get value to the customer as quickly as possible**
2. **Keep work moving**
3. **Every step adds value**
4. **Smaller batches are better - one-piece flow is best**

We should design services to make work flow. That means work is dealt with as up-front as possible. In service the biggest barrier to flowing work is dirty information. Many solutions have some sort of cleaning process on the front of the work to ensure that once it is released it will flow smoothly through the rest of the process.

Flow should be one piece at time. Batches of work cause delay in creating, managing and dealing with the flow. Batching is not more efficient. So handle work one piece at a time and keep it in motion, hopefully moving it as little as possible and only through value steps.

For example, it is better to get together all the pieces of information needed for a housing benefit claim before starting the entitlement process. Once started, any rework to loop back and pick up missed information will create delays. The ideal process is where an officer makes contact with the claimants and tells them all the things they need to bring in and then checks that they have brought them. That officer should be the one to process the whole claim and he should do it straight away. That is clean information and one-piece flow.

The work should keep moving. This means that there are no delays or loop-backs in the work. In perfect flow there will be no piles of folders, no work queues in IT systems and no waiting between steps.

Every step should add value. This means that inspection will not exist since inspection or checking of work is not adding anything to the work. Batching and sorting will also be eliminated in a state of flow.

The logical end to eliminating batches is that you have one-piece flow where each piece of work makes its own way through the necessary steps until the work is done. This is especially useful where the variety in the work means that each piece of work takes a different route. Consider an Accident and Emergency department. Every patient that arrives will have a different requirement for treatment, tests, admission and discharge. No two patients will travel exactly the same path. This is true to a lesser extent in many service systems but the flexibility of designing the flows of work means that not bundling work together allows work to find its own most efficient path unencumbered by being part of a batch.

Seeing flow

In manufacturing it is much easier to see flow. The car assembly plants where the cars move slowly along, passing each of the different stations that are needed to put the car together are an example where the flow is obvious. The car keeps moving, having parts added until it gets to the end of the conveyor.

In services, flow is much harder to spot. We often resort to looking for the lack of flow. This can be useful since if you see batches of work or work waiting then that will point up areas that can be improved. But the real benefit comes when you can redesign processes to flow from end to end with flow built in. Simply patching flow onto an existing process can bring some gains but it is the reworking from beginning to end with the reason for the service and flow in mind that gives the most amazing results.

False flow

Beware of false flow where work moves to the next step when it is not ready. This can sometimes happen when people take too much notice of concepts like takt time. Takt time is a drumbeat that dictates the time it takes to complete a step. It is normally derived from the demand coming in versus the time taken to complete each process step. The mistake made is that people take these calculations too literally and say that step 6 must take 20 minutes and so the work must move on after the 20 minutes allotted and that any work not completed will be sorted later. That is not flow; that is rigidity in process. That kind of mistake will reduce flow. The work has to come back eventually and depending what has been missed, it may very well slow down or block subsequent process steps. What should happen is that the variety in the work is accounted for in the process. When the temptation arises to pass along incomplete work, it is time to ask why and solve the problem so that situation never arises again. Sticking to calcified process definitions is an anathema to continuous improvement.

Pull only if you can't flow

If you can't have flow, you should pull. This is where a process step will pull from the previous step the things it needs to get the job done. Instead of a big planning mechanism directing work, each step communicates with the previous and the next via pull mechanisms.

A nice example of a pull system is in supermarkets. When a can of beans is taken from a shelf to the cash register, a signal is sent to the warehouse that another can of beans is needed on the shelf. The removal of that can from the warehouse in turn pulls from the distribution hub, which in turn pulls from the baked bean manufacturer.

Often IT systems are used to direct the work to be done next; sometimes this is done by some sort of supervisor. This is too complex and the planning mechanism will break down as errors, delays and rework creep in. By pulling from the previous step the need for this massive planning is removed.

If we again imagine the can of beans we can see that a massive system to predict, plan and manage baked bean sales, warehousing and manufacturing would be very complex to build and run. But with each step pulling from the last, the system will manage itself, eliminating a lot of the complexity.

Pull is not an end state. People get very proud of their pull mechanisms, but the desired state is for work to flow without stopping. Move from pull to flow as soon as you can.

False pull

Pull can be confusing. Because it is necessarily an in-process trigger, people sometimes mistake an elegant pull process for a good process. They think that a process step pulling from the previous step is necessarily a good thing all the while forgetting that it is customer value that should define the process.

Again a good example is Accident and Emergency. I once had a hospital manager try to convince me that patients should wait in A&E until wards were ready and the ward could pull the patient to the ward. The manager had a nice mechanism that would have a junior doctor come down to assess the patient then report back to the ward on their status after which the ward team would inform A&E when they were ready to receive the patient. The manager even went so far as to imply that wards might not take patients even when they had spare beds because having too many patients would reduce the time with current patients and reduce the learning that occurred on the ward. Thinking about this from the patients' point of view would quickly raise the point that the hospital is not there for the convenience of the doctors, but there to give the right treatment to the patient at the right time. If the patient has come to A&E then the right time is most likely as soon as possible.

You can still apply a notion of pull, but it is not that the ward is pulling from A&E, it is that the patient is pulling treatment toward them. The onus is then on the ward to understand the demand from A&E so that when a patient pulls the need for a bed, the ward has the capacity to provide it straight away. Yet another way of thinking about it is that from arrival at A&E the patient flows smoothly through any and all steps to be treated and discharged. If one of the steps is to spend some time in a ward bed, the patient should flow smoothly to there too.

It is the rigorous application of flow, pull and value, which will reduce each patient's stay on the ward, which will in turn increase the capacity of the ward to accept new admissions. Improvement begets improvement.

Chapter 6
Problem solving with HELP

Organisations need to develop problem solving skills in order to improve.

Staff need to know how to solve problems, investigate possible improvements, run experiments and evaluate the results. Management need to learn to stop trying to solve the problems themselves, get out of the way and then support the staff in their efforts.

The most important thing in the new way of thinking about problems is that we learn from mistakes.

Types of errors

Russell Ackoff describes two types of mistakes:

1. **Errors of commission – where we do something wrong**

2. **Errors of omission – where we fail to do something that should have been done**

Ackoff says that when we do something right, we learn nothing. If we already know how to do a task and we do it that way and it turns out fine, we haven't added anything to what we know. It is only when we err that learning takes place.

We learn more from errors of commission than from errors of omission. We gain knowledge by trying things and messing them up. We learn nothing when we don't try anything new. We don't learn tennis by not playing; we learn by playing badly at first and noting what we need to do differently the next time we strike the ball.

An example of an error of omission is when Kodak didn't move into digital technology as they watched their competitors change their businesses. They did nothing since they didn't want to take the risk of changing too early. Eventually they had to change, but the mistake of inaction cost them first-mover advantage and they needed massive investment to catch up in a short time.

Errors of omission are more common than errors of commission since it is much easier not to act than to take a risk in being wrong. The irony is that errors of omission are very hard to track and measure, because recording a lack of action is very hard.

Errors of commission are more public and in the modern world are frowned upon. Examples could be miscalculating benefits entitlement or completing a repair to a poor standard.

Doing something right teaches nothing

The common mode of management is to reward for doing a good job. This often means a reward for doing the job as currently specified. If people toe the line and do as they are told, then they are praised or otherwise rewarded for that conformance. This is rewarding inaction. Of course there is action – they are doing their work – but there is no new action to change things. In this case we are rewarding the status quo. Not trying something new is being rewarded. This tells staff it is better to get your head down and do what has always been done and you will be recognised for that. This is an easy course and staff will take it if it is offered.

Instead we should stop rewarding staff for just doing their job and start encouraging them to try new things. We need to support this and provide resources.

It is tempting to suggest that we should reward this effort, but in fact rewards can be sub-optimal in themselves. See Chapter 9 for more on intrinsic versus extrinsic motivation. Suffice it to say that trying something new, learning from it and then seeing the improvement is sufficient reward for anyone.

People avoid the risk of error

People avoid acting because they think that inaction means never being wrong. Avoiding action, except for doing things you already know how to do, means you stop learning.

In many organisations a strong blame culture is present, which means people are afraid of erring in public since they know they will be singled out for a dressing down and made to feel foolish. Hence, nobody tries anything new and the organisation as a whole stops learning.

How risk averse is your organisation?

Are people learning by trying things or are they afraid of what might happen if they do?

The problem is that managers and staff don't know how to fail. Failure should be embraced as part of the learning process and hence supported and encouraged.

It is important to understand that we are not talking about catastrophic failure. Nobody is suggesting that we can bring down the organisation and simply chalk it up to experience. The failures meant are small failures in a controlled environment. There is a way to fail that maximises learning and means that nothing truly bad happens.

Most managers don't know how to experiment with new ideas, some of which will fail. The key is to set up the trial or experiment in a systematic way such that the failure is limited and the learning maximised whatever the outcome.

In short, organisations, managers and staff need to learn how to learn.

Plan, Do, Study, Act revisited

Walter Shewhart first described the idea, test, evaluate, implement sequence that we know as the Plan, Do, Study, Act (PDSA) cycle in the 1920s when he worked for Bell Labs.*

The Shewhart cycle (also known as the Deming cycle) is actually the scientific method.

Scientific method

The process of science is a simple one. You come up with a hypothesis – something you think is true about the world. You then design an experiment to test that hypothesis. The results of the experiment teaches you about the correctness or otherwise of your hypothesis. You can then change your theory that will in turn suggest a new hypothesis. So around the cycle you go again and scientific knowledge advances.

Focused experiments

The experiment is designed such that it is only testing that hypothesis and that, as far as possible, all variables apart from the one in question are kept constant. For example, a classic school physics experiment is to test one of the Gas Laws, the Pressure Law (or Gay-Lussac's Law). The hypothesis is that the pressure of a gas is proportional to the temperature of the gas. The experiment is simple; you have a closed container with a pressure gauge and a thermometer and you vary the temperature and measure the pressure in the container. It is essential that the volume in the container is constant throughout the experiment since changing the volume will also affect the pressure.

In the real world we are not dealing with laboratory conditions, but it is still important to hold constant or to allow for other variables while we test the one in question. There are libraries full of books on just this

---

*Plan, Do, Study, Act (PDSA) is sometimes referred to as Plan, Do, Check, Act (PDCA).

question, but I thought it important enough to spell out the principle lest it went unmentioned and uninformative or, worse, incorrect conclusions were taken from badly thought out experiments.

Old acronym not helpful

When introducing PDSA to clients I have changed the words I use since Plan, Do, Study, Act is a little confusing. People always seem to think that "Plan" is a massive exercise in planning, with projects and documents and whatnot. It is simply a hypothesis with a way of testing it. "Do" is confused with actually implementing the whole plan and can cause people to jump to full implementation without actually testing their idea. "Study" is therefore often missed and people don't really have any idea of "Act", when of course it should be where we either implement the idea or don't, depending on the outcome of the experiment.

You might hear that the "Plan, Do, Check, Act" cycle can be collapsed into "Check, Plan, Do"* but this misses the essential point that it is impossible to start at Check even if you wanted to. The Plan step is logically unavoidable since you must have some tacit hypothesis about what you are going to check first. Also as you go round the cycle the Do phase has to double for the part where you test and the part where you put what you learn into practice. It is important to separate the experiment phase from the put into practice phase since it is the experiment phase where you can try different ideas and take a flyer on new ways of thinking. Having to enact or not with no experimental phase will only constrain the ideas that people suggest.

The phases have been renamed to bring them back into line with the scientific method, making it clearer what should be done in each stage. It is my experience with clients that this new acronym is more effective.

---

*Brian Joiner in *Fourth Generation Management* (1994) or John Seddon in *Freedom From Command and Control* (2005).

HELP

The new version is HELP.

♦ **Hypothesis**

♦ **Experiment / Examine Data**

♦ **Learn**

♦ **Put into Practice**

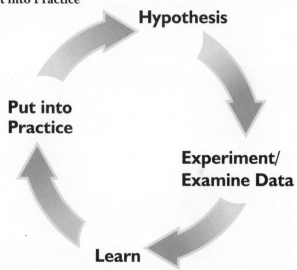

Missed appointments

There is an interesting example from a study[*] in a group of GP surgeries in Bedfordshire where they were having problems with patients not turning up for appointments. Obviously this was a huge waste since the doctors' time was underused and there were patients who could have used those appointments who were being made to wait.

The study applied the principle that promises and pledges that are clearly and voluntarily stated can make people act more reliably. Part of the study involved receptionists taking a call for an appointment and asking the patient if they would be willing to call if they had to cancel, and then leaving a pause to allow the patient the opportunity to reply,

---

[*]Study was by NHS Bedfordshire, BDO and Influence at Work. More at http://www.mindspace-online.org/?p=158

"Yes." The patient was also asked to verbally repeat back the time and the date of the appointment whilst still on the phone.

According to the study, this alone caused the no shows to fall by 6.7%.

This was combined with other ideas. They changed signs in the surgery to be more positive. Instead of a sign reading "67 Patients Failed to Attend Their Appointments Last Month" they changed it to read "94% of Our Patients Attended Their Appointment Last Month". Also nurses asked patients to fill in appointment cards themselves instead of the nurses doing it.

The combination of all these ideas saw a drop in missed appointments of 30%.

These are simple, no or low cost ideas that had a clear and elementary way to test them. They showed significant results and were easy to implement.

The important thing is that if you read that example and think that it might apply to your service, don't just copy it. Follow the HELP method and design an experiment to test it for yourself. Remember, the adding of the question at the end of each appointment call added another few seconds to that call. If doing that doesn't work in your service then blindly adding that question will increase the receptionist's time on the phone, introducing waste.

It also might be that the principle works for you but you need to run a series of experiments to find the best question. The ones in the example may or may not work well, if at all.

It is instructive to note that in the Bedfordshire study, the first thing they tried was to ask people calling for appointments to write down a 4-digit appointment identification number. That caused no shows to rise by 1.1%. They didn't give up after that and went on to discover the things that produced the 30% fall as described.

The base principle here is to use the HELP method to ensure that you have tested ideas in a methodical way before implementing them.

Trial and error

The core of implementing HELP successfully is that you employ trial and error. This requires that you accept that some of the experiments will fail. However, if the HELP cycles are implemented diligently then it is never true that a cycle has actually failed. It may be that a HELP cycle shows that the hypothesis is wrong, but if new lessons are learned which guide the creation of the next hypothesis, then there is no failure. So we can amend our need for the acceptance of failure to be the need for the acceptance of temporary incorrectness on the path to improvement and learning.

A paper exercise is just that

It is useful to reiterate, since it is so important, that taking action solves problems. Don't let the Hypothesis stage of HELP become the bottleneck in the cycle. A clearly stated hypothesis with a solid description and a reliable way of measuring the outcome is sufficient. Do not go down the route of cost/benefit analysis or large project plans.

Adapt - successful failure

In telling the story of a Russian engineer, Peter Palchinsky, in the book *Adapt: Why Success Always Starts with Failure,* Tim Harford describes the three principles to successful failure:

1. **Diversity - try lots of different types of ideas**
2. **Fail small - don't get wiped out by one experiment**
3. **Quickly see the difference between failure and success**

And we can add one more:

4. **Keep going**

Diversity

Diversity means that we try lots of different avenues to solve a problem. We don't decide that any one method or way of thinking is the one true way. We let different people try different things in different ways, all on a small scale to decide what suits us best.

Strange as it sounds, Tim Harford writes in *Adapt* that Winston Churchill, of all people, was sceptical about the Spitfire fighter plane. However, the British Air Ministry had a civil servant called Air Commodore Henry Cave-Browne-Cave who used the flexibility in the procedures to fund the development of the Spitfire calling it a 'most interesting experiment'. Even with doubts, diversity was encouraged which let the Spitfire be developed and later go on to play its crucial role in the Battle of Britain.

Fail small

It is essential that the downside of our experiments is limited. This means small scale, short time and the minimum risk to resources. Thus if the hypothesis is shown to be incorrect, the learning that results occurs at a reasonable cost.

Connecting for Health is the huge NHS project to put patient records in an electronic format which after many years has now all but ground to a halt. It would have benefited greatly from more piloting in a couple of acute trusts and a handful of GP surgeries. In this way the concept could have been tested, the bugs ironed out and the delivery method assured in months and in a small area. Instead it slowly failed over years on a national scale, costing billions.

Distinguish failure from success

Of all the three principles on Tim Harford's list, this is the hardest. The ability to know when a method needs to be dropped and another tried is something of a subtle skill. It requires self-confidence to eliminate a course of action that you yourself have suggested and not to defend it. It takes good design of the Experiment section of HELP to ensure that the evidence is as clear as possible.

This is a Goldilocks problem to which there is no clear-cut answer. We need to drop bad ideas as quickly as possible, but not drop ideas so fast that we fail to give them a proper chance to prove themselves. We need to get the balance 'just right'.

Keep going

Applying HELP requires tenacity and discipline. Others in the organisation, at all levels, will not be comfortable with the failures that are happening. It takes determination to push past, learn, and to keep reapplying and creating experiments to learn anew after having to explain to your manager for the umpteenth time that, "We learned something from that and it gave us some even better ideas to try next."

The practicalities of HELP are explained more fully in the Take Action section in Chapter 23.

Ask "Why?" five times

The other thing to consider before you run your experiment is have you got the best hypothesis? The easy trap to fall into is to treat symptoms and not root causes.

The easiest way to avoid this is to use the "5 Whys" or to ask why five times.

When someone comes up with a hypothesis ask if there is something that underlies it. Ask, "Why?" Then if a deeper cause is uncovered, again ask why that is the case and so on until you get to the root cause of the problem.

An example of the 5 Whys:

> **Why did that person call?** – *She was complaining that she hadn't got the letter we promised to send.*

> **Why didn't she get the letter?** – *When we rechecked her address, we had taken an invalid postcode.*

> **Why had we taken an invalid postcode?** – *We don't check postcodes against the national Postcode Address File database.*

> **Why don't we check against the national database?** – *We assumed it was too expensive.*

> **Why did we assume that?** – *We have never studied wasteful contacts caused by incorrect postcodes before.*

> **Outcome** – *A hypothesis stating that we can reduce wasteful contacts by checking postcodes against the national database.*

Contrast that with not asking why at all where we simply send the customer another letter, which of course, will still have the incorrect postcode.

The number five is not a strict thing. People get hung up about these things when in fact it is important to understand the principle. The point is not to ask why exactly five times, but to ask why enough. People rarely ask why at all, so to suggest that five is a good number is simply pushing them to look deeper. It may be that four or three or two is sufficient depending upon what you are studying at the time.

It is also important not to ask why too many times. If you get to a situation where you are asking about why some road repairs take longer than others you might come up with the answer that the weather stops work. If you were to proceed to ask why storms happen then you are going too far since the occurrence of storms is obviously outside of your control.

The extent of the investigation should stay within the sphere of reasonable influence but go as far as is needed to illuminate the root cause.

There also may be multiple root causes. We must ensure that we ask sufficient questions around the topic to ensure that we don't just alight on only one of many possible reasons for a symptom.

Behavioural pressures

As you ask why, you are likely to come upon behavioural pressures.* These are situations caused by policy, management style, targets, inspections, etc. They are not simply process changes that can be implemented; they will have to be escalated up to higher management or in extreme cases outside the organisation to auditors, government or other outside bodies. In the most awkward cases the behavioural pressure may be legislation.

There is more detail about behavioural pressures in Chapter 16, but suffice it to say here that upper management will have to support the team by using their influence to get these bigger changes implemented.

It is in these situations that a really solid implementation of HELP can really work wonders. A clearly stated hypothesis, a solid experiment with clear learning and a plan to put it into practice will make persuading the powers that be that much easier.

Problem solving is improvement

When an organisation puts into place a sustained programme of staff solving problems, supported by their managers who are in turn properly resourced by upper management, they will find that improvement will accelerate.

There is always talk of the law of diminishing returns in improvement. This law does not exist. The reason is that as small areas are tidied up, that lifts the view to bigger systems, and if upper management are doing their job, they will already have this view and their co-ordination will

---

*Behavioural pressures are another name for "system conditions"
as described by John Seddon in *Freedom From Command and Control* (2005)

bring together the smaller improvements so that larger scale jumps in performance can be made.

It is always hoped that improvements on a whole system level will be made first. The situation in practice is that, to use an analogy, you have to tidy the room before you can decorate. You have to clear the local systems before you can attack the system as a whole. The saving grace is that this does accelerate as people in an organisation at all levels get more experience.

Section 2

People

Chapter 7

Good culture comes from good work

Teamwork comes from achieving goals.

Many artificial methods are employed to try and get teams to work together. Organisations send their staff on motivational courses, have team development trainers come in to play games with groups and have a myriad of personality profiling techniques deployed.

Listening to motivational speakers and playing games will do nothing to improve team performance if that team arrives back to do the same work. In fact, the promise of working better together followed by the disappointment of coming back and being stopped from making any material change will make staff more frustrated than they were before they set off for the training. The money spent on the time out with no real payoff causes further frustration.

Some aspects of profiling can be useful, since it is always interesting to know what people's interests, aptitudes and individual goals are. But it is taken much too far and is marginal in comparison to the power of examining the system, changing it to give better service to the public and doing it together in a natural way.

A meaningful goal is the thing to beat

Once the reason for the system is clear, customer value is understood and the current performance is plotted, there is a clear goal for the team to work together to move towards.

With the subjective targets gone and a solid HELP method to follow, the task of working as a team is much simpler. Foggy goals are the bane of good team working since everyone will be doing their own thing. Their efforts will inevitably be at cross-purposes to the goals of other individuals, those of the team and the system as a whole.

Achieving the goals of increasing customer value and reducing variation in delivery will bring a team together.

People don't like to compete

People much prefer to work together to achieve goals. No one really likes to compete, even the winners and certainly not the losers.* There is an unspoken acceptance of competition in western societies as the default mode of operation, even though it has been shown to degrade performance and make people unhappy.

It is strange that in an arena like public services where you would predict that there would be more co-operation, the default of competitive action still applies. People still compete for budget, status and power, and when things go wrong people compete to avoid blame.

Competition is forced on public sector bodies by policies like league tables where schools, hospitals and other bodies are ranked by their conformance to targets. As we will see, targets are subjective, people cheat

---

*Kohn, Alfie. *No Contest: The Case Against Competition,* Houghton Mifflin (1993)

and the wrong things are measured. League tables force organisations to distort the system in an attempt to rise up in the rankings.

Stating the reason in terms of what is valuable to the public, then working to increase that value and the speed it is delivered, is very satisfying to those who work in the public sector. It is doing what they came to do – to help, to give back – and doing it better than they imagined and with a method to continue to improve.

Trying to better ourselves

It is personally satisfying to do a better job.

As a student I worked for three consecutive years, over Christmas breaks, doing night shifts for the Royal Mail. I hand sorted letters and packages and one year ran the huge automated sorting machines, picking torn letters from the mechanism to try and keep the machine running. Even though the work itself was really boring, I got through the night by trying to do the work as well as I could. When working on the machines, it was a matter of personal pride that I could keep the sorting machines running for 5 minutes without a jam, and when I was hand-sorting letters, if I managed four boxes one hour then it was a personal challenge to sort four and a half boxes in the next hour.

This was a way to keep myself entertained since improving, even on such a mundane task, is interesting and it meant that the otherwise long night shifts would go past a little quicker.

You can imagine how good I felt when a permanent member of staff came past one night and saw me sorting and said, "Slow down son. You are making the permie posties look silly."

Trying to better the team

Personal mastery is something to strive for, but since we are social animals, being a part of a smoothly running team is one of the most fulfilling things we can experience. The biggest pleasure that I get as a consultant is seeing what starts out as just a bunch of people turn into a team and then into a performing team.

They can do it because they concentrate on the work and they are working together, supporting each other, towards a common purpose, not because they have been put through a simulation in a training room.

Trying to better the system

There are also those amongst us that also take pleasure in a well-oiled mechanism. Staff are part of a system and having that system work well is a joy to watch. There is an intellectual pleasure in the mechanics of work. Solving the problems of how many people, in what steps, are needed to deliver value is tremendously satisfying. Working together to solve those problems, to see the system meshing nicely together every day is rewarding. Some people strive for this as an end in itself. Married with a well-directed reason, this is a powerful drive to have as part of your team.

The reason drives the work

The bottom line is that if your reason for highway maintenance is to keep the roads in good repair, then achieving that will be reward enough. Ensuring that the public is getting the best service is why we are here. The spin-off benefits of budget savings and eliminating annoying wasteful contacts are great, but delivering against the reason is a fantastic feeling.

Knowing what needs to be achieved means knowing what to do

Stephen Covey writes about starting with the end in mind.[*] A reason based on what is valuable to the customer is just that. We know what

---

[*]Covey, Stephen. *The 7 Habits of Highly Effective People,* Simon & Schuster Ltd (2004)

we want to achieve and we can then work backwards to first see how well we deliver against that and then how to redesign the work to achieve it.

The improvement tasks need to be broken down into steps and implemented in chunks. You can do as many in parallel as you see fit but without overloading the team. It is suggested that you let the change evolve naturally as people see things to improve. Forcing project structures on a team can take them back to the old days where the corporate way of doing things prevailed and the projects and programmes got in the way of the work and serving the public.

Knowing what to do means knowing what to try

Once we know what we have to achieve, it can guide us in what HELP cycles to try. Starting with the end in mind will give us the intermediate steps, but then we need to test those steps and HELP is the way to do it.

Chapter 8
People want to do a good job

At the heart of the

human psyche is a desire

to do things well.

In Daniel Pink's recent book, *Drive,*[*] he describes how it is expected that extrinsic rewards such as pay and bonuses will motivate. Not only do rewards not motivate in the way predicted, they actually make people less able to solve even simple problems because their focus is on the reward. With the same problem and no extrinsic reward, the reward comes from inside and is much more motivating.

Deep down staff want to do well

Do interesting work

Interesting work and problems to solve are the prime motivators after a decent salary is set. Once people don't have to worry about making

---

[*]Pink, Daniel. *Drive: The Surprising Truth About What Motivates Us*, Canongate Books Ltd (2010)

a living, then learning about something complex is one of the reasons why they will jump out of bed in the morning.

There is no doubt that the challenge of not just saving services but improving them while in a period of massive cuts is an interesting problem.

Feel valued

People want to feel valued, and working as part of a team to provide services to the public is a great way to get that.

Achievement

A sense of achievement is a powerful motivator. To feel that you have put your all into a problem, solved it to the best of your ability, that you have contributed and also learned something along the way is a great thing to take home with you.

Do well for colleagues

Be part of a community

Workers everywhere love to feel part of something. For many people work is also their social life; if they can tie them together at work by not only mixing with people that they like but also with people that they bond with because they have a common purpose, that can create more than friends. That creates a community.

Be part of a gang

I recall watching the HBO mini-series *Band of Brothers*,[*] in which the 147 American soldiers of Easy Company fight their way through the Second World War from the Normandy beach landings all the way through to Berlin. Though it was a dramatisation, they would occasionally have some of the actual men who featured in the series telling of their memories. The interview that sticks in my mind is when

---

[*]based on the book: Ambrose, Stephen E. *Band of Brothers*, Pocket Books, (2001)

an old soldier is describing what it is like in the heat of battle. He said, "When they bullets are flying past, you forget flag and country. You are doing it for the man to your left and the man to your right. They are who you fight the hardest for. And they for you."

Want to please their boss

As much as we might mock management, and can tell stories of terrible managers over the years, we all want to do well for our manager. I am still in touch with a couple of my former managers. A good manager can make all the difference.

Doing well leads to promotion and better things

Doing a good job will lead to praise but also the opportunity for better pay, promotion and most importantly more interesting work. When I worked at Chase Manhattan, I improved the profit and loss reconciliation that took three of us 10 hours a day and reduced that to two people taking 2 hours a day. That enabled my supervisor to leave and work in New York and for me to move departments to do more interesting work. If I hadn't strived to improve that work, who knows, I might be there still.

People want to get on, and showing that you don't just do the work well but can bring innovation and skills to improve work will speed you on much faster.

Working for society

The ethos of people in the public sector is that they want to put something back. They have often seen something that could be better in society and they want to do something about it. That might be in the thrill of seeing children learn, caring for the sick or simply providing good services to those who need it most.

Part of a wider community

Working in the public sector means that you feel like part of a wider community. Not just the community at work but that you are tied into society in an important way. The services that you work to provide are there to help the vulnerable and needy, and society hangs together on the work that the public sector provides. This can give a powerful feeling of belonging to something bigger and more important than just us.

The notion of a reason that is the underpinning of this system of improvement is the thing that goes back to this feeling that we are meant to do something that has meaning.

That feeling extends to our children and future generations that will benefit from a good economic situation, educational opportunities for all and the sense that our society looks after those who can't look after themselves.

Chapter 9

Real motivation comes from within

The key to motivation is not to try to motivate people but in fact to stop doing the many things we do to demotivate them.

The normal models of motivation are outdated. As Daniel Pink has written in *Drive* and Alfie Kohn wrote in *Punished by Rewards,*[*] the carrot and stick theory of motivation is all but dead in scientific circles. However, in management it is very much alive and this needs to change before we can really get our organisations moving.

Accepted models of motivation

Carrot and stick

The most common form of motivation is the reward or the "carrot" in the "carrot and stick" model. This takes the form of pay, bonuses, benefits and praise. The carrot is something we want, need or are drawn to. We need a decent rate of pay and of course greater pay means we

---

[*]Kohn, Alfie. *Punished by Rewards,* Houghton Mifflin (2000)

can buy more, so we want that too. Praise is something that we like as well. Being told we are doing a good job is pleasing. More of that is something that most people would approve of.

Carrots reward good behaviour. Run a good project and get a bonus. Turn up every day and get a good attendance award. Work hard and get a promotion.

The stick is the counterpart to the carrot. This is the punishment side. If your work is not so great or plain bad, you make some terrible error of judgement, a normal mistake or perhaps you can't get out of bed in the morning, then there are consequences. You might suffer demotion, the sack, a "lateral move", a telling off, be reported to HR or perhaps you might get less interesting work or projects.

The carrot and stick work in combination. Do well and we will reward you; do badly and you get punished.

Both reward and punishment take the same form: "Do this and get that."

While most managers reserve punishment for extreme cases seeing that acting harshly can backfire, Kohn argues in *Punished by Rewards* that rewards suffer from exactly the same problems as punishments.

Kohn says that the "do this and get that" model ensures that the person is focused predominantly on the "get that" part and not on the "do this". This means that getting the reward becomes the focus rather than doing good work. This is equally true for punishments as it is for rewards.

This has several negative outcomes. The focus on the rewards constrains creativity on the activity at hand, so people don't apply lateral thinking to the work they are doing because they are thinking about the bonus at the end. Risk taking is also limited since the instinct is to play it safe, to avoid censure and get what is wanted. While people show inherent curiosity in interesting problems, as soon as rewards are introduced the intrinsic interest goes away. So if you subsequently remove the reward, less attention will be paid to the work. An example described by Kohn to illustrate the idea is that while all children love to draw, a study found that children rewarded to draw with sweets and praise lost interest in drawing when the rewards were not offered for drawing later. This is also true for work.

In *Drive*, Pink tells the story of the candle problem. A study constructed a situation where people were given a wax candle, a book of matches and an open box of tacks. These were placed on a table by a wall. The task was to attach the candle to the wall so that it was not touching the table.

People usually start by trying to tack the candle to the wall, but this doesn't work. The solution is to realise that the box containing the tacks can have a dual purpose. So you empty the box of tacks and tack the box to the wall and put the candle in the box.

The study paid some people and not others. They found that not only were the unpaid subjects more likely to solve the puzzle than the paid subjects, but even if the paid subjects solved the problem they would consistently take longer than the unpaid subjects who solved the problem. It was as if the reward was constraining thinking and worsening performance.

In *Punished by Rewards,* Alfie Kohn tells of a study where subjects were asked to try to solve a puzzle in a set time. The puzzle was interesting and also impossible to solve in the time given. Some subjects were paid and the rest unpaid. After the time given had elapsed, the subjects were told that the experimenter had to leave the room to prepare the second part of the experiment. In fact the second part was leaving the subject in the room with the unsolved puzzle.

The people offered money to solve the puzzle left the puzzle untouched after being left alone with it. In contrast, the majority of the unpaid subjects would try to finish the puzzle when left alone.

The puzzle was worth doing for the reward, but after the experiment seemed to be over, there was no reason for the paid subjects to try to solve the puzzle. Any intrinsic interest they had had been drummed out of them by the offer of money. The unpaid subjects were still interested in the puzzle and so wanted to solve it for its own sake.

The conclusion drawn is that the performance in more complex tasks is made worse when rewards are offered.

Intrinsic motivation is more powerful

The alternative to carrot and stick is to make the best use of intrinsic motivation. This is the motivation that comes from within to:

♦ **Do a good job**
♦ **Enjoy things that are interesting**
♦ **Help others**
♦ **Take pride in ourselves**
♦ **Take pride in our work**

As W. Edwards Deming said in his 14 points for management, we need to foster "Joy in work".

It is amazing sometimes to see what people do outside of work for no pay at all. They do things like running scout troops, organising football leagues, hosting knitting circles or producing amateur theatre. They help with charities or volunteer in the community for nothing and sometimes at a cost to themselves. People do all this because it is interesting and worthwhile.

You often find that the people who seem least motivated while in work are the most self-motivated in their private and social lives.

If we could harness even part of this intrinsic motivation while staff are at work we could achieve great things.

Basic needs are necessary

We can't ignore the basic needs that people have. They need to be safe and then they need to be decently paid for what they do so they can afford housing, food and provide for their lives and families. We need to do a little more than this, however. Daniel Pink says we need to take the issue of money off the table. This means that we need to pay people enough so they are no longer thinking about how much they are paid. This probably means that we need to pay them at least the market rate for the job.

Another basic need is that there has to be some level of security in their jobs. The level required is the level that is expected. People understand that jobs are not as permanent today as they once were and they also understand that in the climate of cuts that their jobs are even less secure. We just need to ensure that they are not more worried about their job than they should be. Never give people false hope or security; honesty is always the best policy.

Once we have the basic needs taken care of such that staff are not worried about them we can move on to provide the ingredients of intrinsic motivation.

Daniel Pink writes that the ingredients of intrinsic motivation are:

♦ **Autonomy**

♦ **Mastery**

♦ **Purpose**

Autonomy is giving people responsibility for how they do their own work. Management must trust staff to get on with work knowing that that trust will be repaid.

Mastery is the joy of doing work well, of becoming a master at your job. People with the dullest jobs can gain respect by doing them well, and some people who are in hated jobs still love to be good at them.

Work with a **purpose** is the third criterion. This means doing work with a wider meaning that helps others or the environment. A clear reason is one thing we have talked about, and the wider meaning is what the public sector can provide to staff without too much searching compared with those in the private sector.

It is like the fire triangle, which explains that in order to get combustion you need fuel, oxygen and heat. The equivalent in work is that in order to get motivation – fire in the bellies of staff – you need autonomy, mastery and purpose.

Sometimes it seems that staff are being dunked in the motivational equivalent of a bucket of icy water and then managers wonder why they don't spontaneously combust with enthusiasm.

You can't create intrinsic motivation

Because, by definition, intrinsic motivation comes from within, you can't actually create it. You can only create the environment for it to survive and grow. It is just like gardening in the fact that the gardener is not Dr Frankenstein, she does not create life, but she takes seeds and puts them in an environment that will help them thrive.

Stop blocking it

The quickest thing that managers can do to promote intrinsic motivation is to stop blocking it. So that means letting people think for themselves, stopping extrinsic motivation – no more carrot and stick – and letting staff improve their work so they master it and can take pride in that.

One easy way is to stop saying "no". We all say no a lot and we don't realise we are doing it most of the time. Instead of saying no, simply ask some better questions. Find out what the staff are thinking about, really get to understand what they are offering or thinking of changing and why. The HELP structure can assist here. You may be surprised. Often by not saying no and talking more deeply you will realise that there are merits in what is being suggested. It may be that you can take the initial thought and take what is useful and apply that but not all of it. If in the end the idea is not such a good one, the staff will still feel valued since their manager has at least respected them by taking the time to talk it over properly. Remember that we learn through action, so allow people to try out ideas. Even if they don't work out, they will learn something useful. Having more of these kinds of discussions will also help people to communicate future ideas more clearly since they will have had some practice.

Support it when you see it

When you encounter people who are keen to do something different or try something new there is probably some intrinsic motivation driving them. Support it whatever it is. Again, like the gardener, you might need to guide or focus the effort, but to support it is the most important thing.

Let people see the point

Managers need to help people see the point of their work. Working for a reason is very helpful for intrinsic motivation. The process of developing the statement of the reason will help this, as will replacing measures of busyness with measures related to customer value.

Managers should try to communicate with staff how their work and delivery of value to customers is being viewed and valued by customers and by other parts of the organisation. This is trying to give staff a wider view of how they fit into a system. This will help them to suggest improvements that benefit the system and hence the customer, but it will also give them the wider view that is essential to bolster intrinsic motivation.

Don't praise, enquire

False praise is seen a mile off and will do more harm than good.

I was never very good at art while at school and it always seemed that those with natural talent got all the attention from the teachers while those who struggled a little bit just got left to get on with it. I was aged about 14 when we were set homework to draw a still life of some glasses and bottles. I didn't do it properly. I dashed it off on my knee sitting on the bus to school. It was a terrible drawing. When I got my homework back it had been given a B+. I knew it wasn't that good, nowhere near. I waited after class and asked the teacher, who in all other respects was perfectly nice, why she had given me a mark that I didn't deserve. She replied that it was to try to encourage me. I said that encouragement would come from teaching me some more tricks of how to see things and draw them, but grades I didn't deserve meant nothing. She never did devote more time to the rest of the class, perhaps she couldn't. I wasn't encouraged.

Years later I did feel the urge to try art again and I enrolled on an evening class entitled "I Can't Draw". I found that of course, I could draw. In an environment where mistakes were there to learn from, the class criticised each other's work in a positive and supportive way. I learned some techniques that I never learned at school. I also learned that it is better to try, fail and learn from it than to give up; something I knew full well in many other areas of life. I now enjoy sketching as a hobby.

Some managers have got into a habit of giving praise even where it isn't due. They think that they should be positive all the time, and in a way they are right. Being positive doesn't mean constant praise, since this is false; it actually means being positive that there is a germ of good sense in every idea and that positive action will surface those ideas that really do work. It is also being positive that even those things that don't work out will teach us something new.

A more interesting way to boost intrinsic motivation rather than use extrinsic motivation via praise is to use enquiry. Instead of saying "Well done", take a genuine interest. Ask how was it done, why did you do it that way, what did you find challenging and what would you do next time? The time a manager takes to ask these and similar questions will let the staff member know that the manager is pleased, but also interested. A simple "Well done" can be seen as dismissive by some and something to be sought after by others. The dismissed are not really happy and those who seek praise as an extrinsic motivator will suffer the same problems as those who seek more tangible rewards.

When they support each other, support that

As staff become freer to try new methods and some of the old ideas that they weren't able to try for years, they will need to support each other. No change, however small, can be tested, evaluated or implemented by a single person in today's highly connected organisations. Cross-functional, cross-team and cross-departmental support is required. Management needs to be there to facilitate, encourage and support spontaneous collaboration as it emerges. Again, at first, this will be more a case of getting out of the way, but as things develop, management will need to become more active in their support. This might be by providing places and times to communicate and meet both physically and using technology, but mostly it will be by letting staff know that their efforts are valued and that talking and working more closely with colleagues is important.

Chapter 10
The waste of staff potential

We hire the best people we can find, so what happens to all that promise?

We recruit good people

Recruitment is very rigorous these days. Candidates go through multiple filters and tests including submitting CVs, attending several interviews and doing various practical and psychometric tests.

What are we looking for by doing all this?

We look for people who are intelligent and can apply that intelligence to the problems and work of the public sector. This also requires a wide variety of personal and technical skills. We need people who get on with others, can work in a team but are also self-starters who have ideas.

We hire people who are keen to muck in and get things done. We want them to see with fresh eyes, to bring a new outlook and come with experience both from the public sector and also from outside too if possible.

Six months later

If this is how we hire, why do we seem to have such problems with implementing change and bringing in new ideas? Our staff seem to become inculcated to the organisational way. It is they who say, "This is the way we have always done things." They seem to have given up trying to change things for the better. They are downtrodden and have stopped coming up with ideas. People aren't communicating and they are just getting on with their work with no appreciation for a system. Networking is negligible and staff sit in their departmental silos not thinking about the organisation let alone the customer.

Don't believe me? Talk to any manager and they will tell you that their staff are resistant to change and that they need help in getting their staff to do what they want.

People volunteer to work harder for free

These are the same people who do all sorts of things outside of work such as volunteering, running sports teams, doing creative hobbies or running marathons. We know they do these things because we prefer to hire people with active outside interests.

So why is it at work that many people cruise along, not putting their heads above the parapet, just getting on with their work? They are not different people; they are just as intelligent, just as energetic and just as motivated as when they go home, but somehow we lose their motivation when they come into work.

We make them that way

So either we hire badly and we are not getting the keen, intelligent, forward-looking people we think we are, or we are doing something to them after they arrive.

We make them that way. After they arrive they are put to work that is predefined and we expect them to do the job. There is hardly ever a release for all the creativity, intelligence and forward thinking that we hired.

The only way to rectify this is to change the system. In order to see improvement we need to redefine job roles and how they relate to changing the system.

Chapter 11

Job roles must change

To provide the best environment for ideas to thrive, the roles of staff, management and upper management must change.

The current set-up has upper management issuing diktats to their reports, who then decide how the work is done to meet these instructions and in turn instruct the front line staff in how to complete the low-level tasks that are their daily work.

This must change drastically to a system where, given a common reason for delivering customer value that is plainly understandable to all, staff are responsible for how the work is done, management are there to provide support and resources and upper management's role is to have a view of the system and co-ordinate strategy in the wider world.

Staff jobs must change

Currently just "work"

Currently many front line staff simply come in to work every day, do the jobs as described and then go home. The opportunities for suggesting new ideas are few and far between and those who have been in the organisation long enough know it is futile to struggle to be heard, so they no longer try.

Management are so used to staff not suggesting new ways of doing the work that they think it is the staff's fault.

Must change to "work and improve"

It will still be the core role of staff to do the work, but that will be added to. From the role of just "work", it will change to "work and improve". The added responsibility of solving problems, identifying, testing and implementing improvements will change their role. There won't be too much resistance to this since the additional tasks are much more interesting than just doing the work as specified.

Seeing customers served better is much more motivating than doing what staff know is dysfunctional and then having to constantly defend it to the public. For here is the irony: management design of work doesn't function very well and while the staff know this, it is they who get it in the neck from the public when things go wrong.

This new dual role of doing work and improving work will leave staff more motivated because they will create work that is more interesting and meaningful. The added benefit of working more effectively in teams will further motivate staff.

Management must change

Managers assume it is their role to think and the role of the staff to do. The question that I often hear from managers as a symptom of why things aren't going so well in an organisation is, "How do I get them to do what I want?" They sound like dog owners. It is as if managers are dealing with another species that they cannot directly communicate with and if only they could find the right combination of biscuits, whistles and chain jerks everything would be okay.

Design of work

Work is designed with no involvement of staff. Sometimes there are meetings that purport to be a consultation with staff but turn out simply to be a preamble to an announcement of plans that were made way before the meeting.

Management use their experience and intelligence to design work. In some cases these are considerable, but management are distant from the work physically and if they ever did do the work in question, it was a while ago, perhaps many years previously. This causes the work to be designed poorly without immediate and current experience of what is really happening. Often management are surprised or even shocked at what actually happens in order to get work done. This is why asking management how work proceeds is a waste of time and why you must go to where the work is done to unearth the truth.

Check conformance

The role of conformance checking is a common one in management today. A vast amount of time is spent ensuring that staff are sticking to the (badly designed) procedures and scripts. Staff are there to do as they are told and one of the answers to the "How do I get them to do what I want?" question is "Check up on them."

A story I like is about a van full of cargo that arrives at a depot to be unloaded. That day the van driver finds his supervisor there with a clipboard checking that everything is going smoothly. The driver backs the van under the roof and up to the receiving bay as usual. He gets out of the van and starts fiddling with the tyres. The supervisor comes over and tells the van driver to "Stop messing about and get the van unloaded. We haven't got all day". The driver shrugs and sets about unloading the van. As he does so the van gets lighter, the tyres decompress and the van gets wedged under the roof, causing some damage to the roof and the top of the van. After that the supervisor always let the van driver let the tyres down a little before unloading.[*]

---

[*]Note that this ending is unsatisfactory. A proper root cause needed to be found and a more permanent fix put in.

Management will see it as their job to check up on conformance to standards; the very standards that staff need to circumvent to get work done properly. Call centre staff have their calls recorded for quality purposes. These are then randomly selected and listened to, to ensure that the proper script and procedures are followed. In short management treat staff like children.

Management also enforce the measures of busyness.

I know someone who before retirement used to work as an educational welfare officer for the local borough. Part of the job was to periodically visit his allocated primary schools and track down any children who had not attended for a while. It was not uncommon for families to move away from the area or go on long holidays in term time having not informed the school. It was often a simple task to make a couple of phone calls to track down the child, note the circumstances and then proceed to amend the school roll if necessary.

Part of the procedure stated that if the child was found within a week from the officer being notified then that was that. If it took longer than a week, a long form had to be filled in. Most other educational welfare officers would visit their schools, take notes about the non-attending children, move on to their next appointment and do the work of tracking down the children a few days later. Subsequently they would often take more than a week to trace the child and thus spend time filling in the forms. This officer was in the habit of sitting in the school office with access to the admin staff and doing the necessary phone calls right away. He did this because it was easier to find the children if you did it sooner. The trail was warmer.

The upshot of this was since he found the children quicker he had to fill in the forms much less often. One benefit was that he had more time to spend on finding children. You would think his managers would be pleased. Quite the contrary. He was once taken into a room by his supervisor and asked why he never filled in these forms. He explained that he found the children quickly so didn't need to. The supervisor told him that since he never filled out the forms, she had no record of what he was doing on this particular task and she would prefer that he filled them in more often. The officer's supervisor actually wanted him to take longer to locate children so he could fill in more forms, spending more time doing so, so she could have evidence of his busyness.

The officer's manager actually wanted him to do his work less well and with more waste.

Change to support and resource

Management need to drop the idea that they know best and that the key to management is figuring out how to get people to do what you want. To get the best from people, managers need to move to a role where they are supporting improvement activities with enthusiasm, facilitation, time, money and coaching.

Understanding what people need to do their jobs and improve them is key to the new role. Supporting staff to navigate their way through the organisation is the next skill. As everyone gains more of an appreciation of the organisational system as a whole, managers will need to guide staff to know who to talk to and to smooth the way in those interactions. Facilitating and initiating new networking possibilities will figure large in the new management skill set. Instead of looking down and frowning, management will now be looking up and out to see what new opportunities there are for their area and staff to work with others to optimise the system as whole and hence maximise customer value.

Upper management must change

The current perception is that upper management such as chief executives and board members sit very far away from the work. They issue orders from their fabled ivory towers and then become displeased when their directions are misapplied, misunderstood or forgotten.

There is a modern incarnation of this where upper management spend time working on "mission and values". They work on principles for the organisation to follow. I attended a local government conference where the chief executive of a London borough set out the principles that the borough should work to. The trouble was they were all so obvious and banal that they were not worth stating. Do the residents and council workers need to be told to be honest and proud of their borough? Firstly, they know they should be honest already and whether they are proud of the borough depends upon how nice it is and how they are treated when they seek a service from it. Good service means they will be proud.

It should be noted that the values in the "mission and values" statements you often hear from many organisations rarely tie in with customer value. Customer value is much more basic and immediate. They don't ask for philosophy; they want it done quickly and done right first time.

See the system as a whole

The new top priority for upper management is to see the system as a whole. As their reports are busy supporting staff to improve, upper management need to ensure that changes are to the benefit of the whole system and not just in a local area. It is easy for departments to optimise themselves, and upper management having a view of the whole can prevent that.

Support managers in their new role

Upper management are there to do the same for management as management do for staff. They must support and provide resources to enable management to do their jobs.

As upper management are responsible for the system, they are also responsible for the improvement method. The sustainability of the new method is in their hands. The questions of reason, demand, performance and flow are core to the new role of upper management. The importance of these new techniques is high on their agenda since they know that the organisation is, what the organisation does. What it does is the work.

Go to see the work

The first thing that should change is that upper management need to get back to the work. They need to be a visible clue that the work and its improvement are now top of the agenda. The best way to achieve this is to go and see. While there, this is a good opportunity to ask management, in their own environment, how they would like to be supported. What do they need from the chief executive to in turn support their staff? In this economic climate, managers will understand that asking for money will be impossible, but they often want to know more clearly what is happening in the rest of the organisation and outside so they can dovetail efforts in their departments.

Set strategy

Upper management must be seen to have a coherent strategy to move the organisation forward. Forward primarily in the service it provides to the customer, but also forward in the context of other providers, government bodies and agencies. For example the overlap of social care between the NHS and local authorities could be a strategic win for the public sector if the strategy of the two parts could align to provide better service, with less duplication and at lower cost. Such a strategy needs to be co-ordinated at upper management level.

Upper management must support long-term goals that are rooted in service. These goals must be based in reality and come from the ground up, which is why upper management need to get closer to the work done by managers and staff. Upper management need also to know how customers value the service received.

Ending short-term thinking must be the next task of upper management. Too much public sector thought is about just this quarter or this financial year. Upper management are sucked into figuring out how they will make it to the next year with budgets intact. They forget that it is investment in doing better work that will yield the savings required this year and in the future.

Communication

The clear and timely communication of these goals, strategies and alliances is the next role of upper management. As they see the system as a whole, so they must describe it to those who don't have the advantage of the lofty view they behold.

Management want to know what is going on in other departments and too often they find out via the grapevine. Upper management must make it their business to ensure that everyone is abreast of everything that is planned as soon as is practicable. Anything less means that management will misdirect their staff in their improvement tasks and the whole edifice will stand on sandy foundations.

The staff has less need to know the overall picture, but they do have to feel part of something important. The energy and commitment that comes from upper management will be crucial to staff to let them know that management, upper management and the public value their contribution. This will spur staff on to further improvements.

The public need to know what is happening with their services. If they don't, it can damage the services themselves. A good example is walk-in centres that have been set up next to many Accident and Emergency departments. They were partly set up to cope with the demand when GPs started to do less out-of-hours work. The fact is that most of the public don't know that walk-in centres exist and if they do they don't understand what they are for, so they continue to go to A&E. Thus resources have been diverted away from A&E to the walk-in centres, but people are still going to A&E and in ever more numbers since they can't get an out-of-hours service from their local doctor.

Public role must change

The role that the public plays and is expected to play needs to change too. But this change must come about in a more natural way. The public are not under anyone's control, but they can be influenced. The key things are that they must be released from the burden of being expected to manage their own services and they must be encouraged to participate more.

Stop being expected to manage

The public often feel that they end up becoming a de facto manager at the organisations that are supposed to be serving them.

Last time I upgraded my mobile phone, I felt I had become the manager of my own personal complaints resolution department. The upgrade and accompanying contract change did not get implemented properly. This cost me a lot of money in data charges that were supposed to be inclusive. I had to call the company about twenty times and become a local expert in the various departments and their interactions. I am now a go-to person for knowledge of the history of putting business customers onto retail servers and the resultant problems of correcting account records. At no point did anyone at the mobile phone company assume responsibility for my problem. I had to co-ordinate between departments, sometimes giving staff the phone numbers of other staff in the hope that they might talk to each other.

Expect good service

The public should simply get good service and they should come to expect it. In the short term, the number of wasteful contacts will increase since as service levels rise, expectations will go up and the resignation that poor service is the norm will disappear. People will start to complain about mediocre service when in the past they would only complain about extremely bad experiences.

As the public tell us more about errors, we will learn from them. The public will learn that telling us is worth their while since it gets them better service next time around. Currently most people think it is not worth complaining most of the time because nothing will happen.

Two-way communication will erupt where the public and organisations are suddenly learning from each other. This has already started with some new services that enable the public to inform local authorities of problems in their area via their mobile phones and email. These methods will only succeed if organisations both follow up on the information provided and work to prevent these problems occurring in the future.

Summary of role changes

Role	Before	After
Staff	♦ *Do the work*	♦ *Do the work* ♦ *Improve the work*
Management	♦ *Design the work* ♦ *Check up on staff conformance*	♦ *Support staff to improve the work*
Upper management	♦ *Issue orders* ♦ *Manage by reports*	♦ *See the system as a whole* ♦ *Communicate the system view*
Public	♦ *De facto managers* ♦ *Expect bad service*	♦ *Involved in improvement* ♦ *Expect good service*

Form follows function

It is a truism in design that form should follow function. The chairs that look beautiful but you can't sit on may be art, but they are not examples of good design. The same principle holds for the design of work.

In the case of work in the public sector, the function is to maximise customer value. Thus the design of work should follow from that.

Management structures come from the work

Management structures such as how departments are configured, stem from an over reliance on economies of scale, specialisation and historical management decisions. Management needs to be reconfigured to support the work, just as the work is configured to give customer value. This means management becomes more fluid. As demand changes, the work must follow and hence the management needed to support it must also change.

In order that upper management are closer to the work, management needs to become flatter. The responsibility for the design of work, which was previously the job of management, will be given to staff. This makes flattening the organisation easier.

Review

As work changes to deliver value instead of serving targets and standards, so our roles as staff, management and upper management must change too. The change in roles comes from the work and travels upward; no more the top-down implementation of change.

Section 3

Systems in Practice

Chapter 12

Management traps

Modern management has developed many ways to try and improve performance.

Managers are constantly looking for short cuts to improve performance and cut costs. These short cuts are very seductive for the unwary manager. Many of them have become the orthodoxy, which makes them even more widespread, pernicious, damaging and much harder to remove.

System or staff?

Budgets are an output of the system of work. A good system is cheap to run and a bad system expensive due to the wasteful contacts, errors, delays and rework.

Focusing on people means coaching individuals to do better in their work in the hope that lots of individuals doing better will improve the system as a whole. This view shows a lack of understanding of people and systems.

95% from the system, 5% from the people

W. Edwards Deming said that 95% of variation comes from the system. The system here is anything and everything to do with the organisation that is trying to deliver value to the customer.

You can ascertain this for yourself by thinking about anyone in your organisation and listing the things that will affect his or her work for good or for ill and then asking yourself whether it is down to the individual or to the system.

Let us try this exercise for a nurse.

Influence on Work	Individual or System
Team	System
Senior Sister	System
Medical staff	System
Training	System
Prior education	Individual
Hospital culture	System
Ward culture	System
Difficulty of cases	System
Attitude	Individual
Pay	System
Ward utilisation	System
Pressure of cases	System
Relationship with colleagues	System
Other departments (pharmacy etc.)	System
Housekeeping	System
Experience	Individual
Intelligence	Individual

The vast majority of influences are due to the system. We assigned attitude to the individual, but it could be argued that the nurse's attitude is to some extent shaped by the culture in the department and the hospital. Experience and prior education are not easily changed, except by the passage of time in the first instance and a time machine in the second.

So we can see for this nurse, and in fact any person that you might consider, that the vast majority of influences on her work come from the system and not from her.

Another way to do this is to listen to calls that come in to a contact centre and have a team list the possible variables that affect how long it takes to deal with the call. A list similar to that above will be generated that will show that most of the causes of variation are due to the system. Examples are the complexity of the call, the training of the agent and whether the call is wanted or wasteful.

My experience is that about 90% of influences on personal performance are due to the system. So the question has to be asked, why do management work on the people?

There is a huge culture of working on and with individuals to get them to perform better. We send them on time management, assertiveness, team working and leadership courses then they come back to work in the same system that they left, totally unable to implement any of the good things that they might have learned.

I am not against any of those skills being taught; I just don't think it is the most effective thing to start with.

The place to start is customer value and the work that delivers value.

Leave the staff alone. The system of work is the responsibility of management.

Targets

The most ubiquitous technique to shift performance is to set targets.

These can take many forms, e.g.

♦ **The number of items completed in a set time** – *e.g. he must process 40 claim forms per day*

♦ **An increase/decrease by x%** – *e.g. increase profits by 5%; decrease errors by 10%*

♦ **A percentage must be within set limits** – *e.g. 75% of category "A" ambulance calls responded to in 8 minutes*

It is not the ambition to improve that is the problem. It is that setting targets is dysfunctional and subjective.

Targets are dysfunctional

Targets are dysfunctional because as Peter Scholtes said, there are three ways to hit a target:

1. **Distort the system**

2. **Distort the figures**

3. **Improve the system**

Accident and Emergency departments holding patients in ambulances so the clock won't start on the four-hour government target to treat patients is a gross distortion of the system.[*]

Distorting figures is pretty common too. There have been instances of teachers changing pupils' GCSE coursework to make the school look better in league tables.[†]

The last option of improving the system takes effort, dedication, teamwork, creativity and embracing new ideas. It is no wonder that in the face of targets, people opt for the easy road.

---

[*] The coalition government has dropped the four-hour A&E target.
[†] http://news.bbc.co.uk/1/hi/education/6918805.stm

Targets are subjective

Nobody has ever been able to explain a good way to set a target. People talk about taking current performance and adding a bit. This is where you get the "current amount plus 5%" target. Notice that they are always a multiple of 5%. This is just a figure plucked from the air. There is no way there is any managerial, scientific or statistical basis to these types of target.

In an MoD office maintenance service the management divides types of repairs into classes: urgent, important and minor. There is a target to deal with urgent repairs in 24 hours, important repairs in 4 working days and minor fixes in 28 days.

What is found is that what matters to the customer can be completely different from the subjective classifications of management. In the MoD office maintenance service they now ask the customers when they would like to have their repair done and that is when they do it. They have two measures: end-to-end time for customers' requests to do it as soon as possible; and "Did we do it when asked?" for customers who request a particular time that is convenient to them. The mandated classes of repair are ignored in the new system and the customers are much happier this way.

We can see that targets are subjective if we use the understanding of variation due to a system. Let's look again at the performance in processing claim forms:

Number of Claim Forms Processed

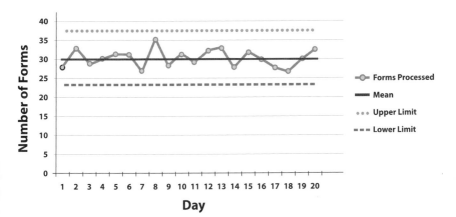

The mean is 30.3, the upper limit is 37.5 and the lower limit is 23.0. We can predict that tomorrow this worker will process between 23 and 38 forms.

With this understanding, how should we set a target? Well if we set a target above the upper limit of 38, say 43 per day, we know predictably that it will not be achieved. If we set the target below the lower limit of 23, say 20 per day, we know that it will always be achieved. What is the point of setting a target that someone will either never or always achieve?

Let us set the target within the limits, say at 30. Well, we know that due to common cause variation in the system, some days the target will be met and some days it won't. The variation in hitting the target is in the system, not due to the worker. Setting a target that is hit randomly is not only fruitless but also annoying.

We can't set the target above, within or below the limits. So there is nowhere that is useful to set it. Therefore, we should not set one at all. Instead we should work with the worker and his colleagues in the rest of the system to improve it as a whole to deliver customer value. Only then will we see a reduction in variation and an increase in the number of forms processed.

Targets are unambitious

Targets are mostly very unambitious. The performance you would get by maximising customer value and minimising waste are way beyond what anyone would set as a target. Back to the office maintenance service where they are getting 100% of the "do it at the customer's convenience" jobs done on the day requested and the "do it as quickly as we can" jobs done in 6 days.

The 28-day target for minor jobs seems completely tame put up against the actual performance they are now getting.

The irony is that they are still measured against these targets. They are doing brilliantly against the 28-day target but worse for the 24-hour and 4-day targets for urgent and important repairs since sometimes the customers want the repairs done later at their convenience and the targets don't cater for that.

Better than targets

A government department commissioned me to do a cost/benefit analysis of the option of sending more of their annual return form processing to an outsourcer. The benefits they predicted were vastly outweighed by the option of bringing the work back in-house. This was mainly owing to the fact that they were going to outsource a waste filled process with no changes. When we walked the flow of work we found that there were 34 steps, 3 of which had value.

Targets squash ambition

There is a tendency to take these very unambitious targets and then meet them by one of the three methods described above and then do nothing further. It is very common that you will see sets of figures that all lie just the right side of the target without exceeding it. It is as if rather than pushing performance, the target actually sets a ceiling.

One of the targets for the ambulance services is that 75% of category A calls are responded to in 8 minutes. Here are the figures for 2008/09 for services across the country:[*]

Ambulance Service NHS Trust	% cat A calls in 8 mins
South Western	78.01%
East Midlands	76.03%
North East	75.69%
London	75.55%
West Midlands	75.40%
South East Coast	75.15%
East of England	74.60%
North West	74.31%
South Central	72.63%
Yorkshire	69.44%
Great Western	68.37%

[*] Sourced from the Care Quality Commission web site at
http://www.cqc.org.uk/publications.cfm?fde_id=13183

The distribution of these figures seems odd. Why are 7 of the 11 trusts only 1% away from the target of 75%? The biggest difference is 6.6% and that is the worst performing trust according to the target, not the best. I would strongly suspect that these services are designed to meet the target as opposed to give the best service to the public.

Services are designed to conform to targets. This is entirely natural. If someone in authority tells you that hitting the target is acceptable, then once you had hit it why would you bust a gut to go further? There is also often a pressure to not exceed targets and quotas in order to prevent embarrassment to others.

The other reason to not exceed a target by too much is that everyone knows that next year there will be a new target. If every year they want an extra 5% on whatever you achieved last year, it is natural to leave room for yourself to achieve that next target. Do too much this year and you will have no slack to be able to make up the gap next year.

A good friend of mine works as a technical salesman and a couple of years ago he told me that in the first quarter he had already made his sales quota for the whole year. I asked him if he was going to motor on and smash all the records by repeating that in the remaining three quarters. He replied, "Don't be silly, they'd only want even more from me next year!" He fully intended to rest on his laurels on just over tickover for the rest of the year. Who can blame him?

Targets demotivate

Targets are supposed to be motivational. They are a challenge. In fact they are just the opposite. Targets are seen as an obstacle to good work and something to be worked around. The subjective nature of targets is also a reason that they are not liked as well as the fact that they offer no method for achieving them. Without method and support, targets are just a way to beat people.

Design of work

Work is designed away from where it is done. This is the cause of much dysfunction.

Upper management don't see the consequences

The central planners and upper management who design the system of work have often never done the work they are designing or they did it so many years ago that they are out of touch with what really goes on. Hence when they make changes, inevitably without talking to staff, the staff are incredulous about what is going on.

Local control over what is happening should not threaten upper management since they would still have the job of strategy and of having the whole system view of the organisation.

See things by documentation

Upper management will often only see what is happening on the front line by reading reports that have filtered up the hierarchy. The reports are written to please the manager above and don't reflect the real goings on. This reflects the view that upper management don't have the time to spend with the staff doing the work. The organisation is what its staff does, and therefore there is no time wasted in upper management spending time in the work.

Intelligence is not enough

Upper management are undoubtedly intelligent and experienced. If they weren't they would not have reached their positions. The problem comes when the professional managers reach executive roles by dint of being good at climbing the ladder rather than because they have knowledge and skills in the sphere of the organisation that they are now managing.

What is needed to rectify this situation is not to dismiss all upper management and replace them with nurses and bin men but to channel that ability into improving the work. This must be done by bringing the work closer to upper management and upper management closer to the work. Only by experiencing what is done and going to see what happens on the ground can upper management maintain a valid view of the system as a whole. We are not talking here about state visits where chief executives, like the Queen, think that the world smells of fresh paint, but of genuine enquiry and support for those who manage and do the work that make the organisation what it is.

Current design is done by very few people

Another aspect of the design of work done by management is that too few people are involved and those people, as discussed already, are not familiar with the day-to-day problems and tasks that are faced. The scope for bringing staff into the decisions about how work is designed simply to increase the number of voices is very great. Many hands make light work. The same is true of design as it is of physical work. The trick is to avoid design by committee. The way to do that is by having a clear reason for the service and understanding of the value to the customer. This will provide the laser focus needed to keep the discussions succinct and productive. This will be most effective if staff from the core work lead the design effort, and support services are pulled in as necessary.

This discussion never really ends since as the HELP process is applied thousands of times, the work will evolve and occasionally make jumps. Supporting the HELP process is one of the ways that upper management and management can get back into understanding the work and its outputs. The Learning and Put into Practice phases can inform management as well as the staff that are running the HELP cycles.

Consensus grows

Involving more people, especially staff, will grow a consensus about what is important. It makes people feel involved and committed if they have had a say and more so if they can take action. It is action that changes minds not words. People remember more of what they do than of what they hear. So taking new methods on board is much more successful if people take part rather than just hear about it.

Lots of little improvements

Using the HELP technique will pull everyone together as team members assist colleagues to move forward. Teams will help other teams to implement cycles since the silo nature of current organisations will need to be straddled to make significant improvements. Recall that systems improve most effectively in the interactions between the parts rather than in the improvement of the parts separately.

Design without evidence

Work is often designed without evidence. Governments have often talked of basing policy on evidence when often the reverse is true. The problem is that either we get suckered into a massive statistical belch that tells us nothing or we are just guessing based on our experience or intuition. W. Edwards Deming said, "Experience is no substitute for knowledge."

The reason that many statistics can be misleading is that we are often measuring the wrong things such as busyness and conformance to targets.

Many of the new principles in this book are counter-intuitive. With evidence and a solid HELP cycle to show it, nothing is counter-intuitive for long. Think it, try it and prove or disprove it. The alternative is intellectual posturing and guesswork.

Blind application of tools

There are thousands of management and improvement tools. Six Sigma teaches over seventy statistical tools that you can apply. Lean adds on yet more tools such as kanban, 5S, poka-yoke, work cells, value stream mapping and many more.

All these tools are useless unless you understand the problems you are facing.

The most important thing to remember about these tools is that they were developed to solve someone else's problem at some other time. If you can identify that you have the exact same problem, then go ahead and apply the tool.

The problem comes when people pick up a bag of tools and start applying them without this understanding.

Actually understanding tools means not only do you have to understand your own problem; you have to understand the other organisation's problem and how the tool resolved it (if it did). That is a lot of work. Stick to your own problems. Fix them using your newfound problem-solving skills and HELP cycles.

Misapplication of 5S

A very common example of misplaced tool application is 5S. Lean programmes often mistakenly start with 5S. 5S is a system to tidy up.

The meanings of the S's are:[*]

♦ **Sort – throw away things you aren't using**

♦ **Straighten – put everything in its proper place**

♦ **Shine – clean everything**

♦ **Standardise – standardise work practice**

♦ **Sustain – implement a way to keep the above
   S's going in the future**

What I often see, especially in the NHS, is before and after photographs of 5S implementations. So you see pharmacy cupboards, supplies rooms and waiting areas that were messy and dirty, all cleaned up and tidy. When asked how that improved patient care, dropped waiting times or sped patients through their treatments, the answer comes back – it didn't. If that is true then they are missing the point. The reason is that there is a misunderstanding about what 5S is for and why it was developed.

5S comes from manufacturing and it is about revealing flow, or the lack of it. In a factory, if there are boxes, tools and work in progress lying

---

[*]You may see slightly different S's used, but they mean the same thing.
Also some people talk about 5S+1 or 6S where the extra S is safety.

around workstations and all over the factory floor it makes it very hard to see if the work is moving through the factory. Get rid of mess, tidy up, clean the place and keep it that way and you have a fighting chance to see the flow of work.

When a clinic in the NHS clears up its cupboards or waiting rooms it is not exposing flow or lack thereof, it is just tidying up. Of course it is slightly nicer to have a clean room to wait in, but the problem is not how pleasant the room is, but the fact that you have to wait at all.

Before 5S is applied, people have to decide whether they have a problem seeing the flow of work in their system and then if 5S will help them with that problem. Most of the time the NHS and the majority of other service providers don't understand their system or customer value, so starting by tidying up won't get them off to a very good start.

Study tools to learn approach to problem solving

We can learn something from tools that come from other organisations and sectors. The thing we can try to learn is the thinking process that led them to that tool. The tool itself is a red herring.

We should learn to "think like they think", but not to "do as they do".

Deming said we must avoid copying at all costs. Management love packages, tools and programmes, but we must avoid them since they all solve other people's problems. We must learn to solve our own.

Multiple customers

How do we deal with the situation where we have multiple customers? Perhaps we are in a support service such as an internal help desk or we have to pander to the needs of politicians, investors, senior management, co-sponsors and others.

Internal customers

Internal customers are a red herring. People speak of upstream providers and downstream customers. This mislabelling of parts of your system as customers will lead to local optimisation that will, in the longer term, sub-optimise the system as a whole. The only customer is the end customer. All steps and processes should be improved to better serve the end customer. It comes back to the difference between efficiency and effectiveness. Is the process step effective in adding value for the customer? If it is not, no matter how efficiently it serves the next step or does its job according to a specification, it needs to be changed, improved or eliminated.

For example, think of an accounts department that is very efficient at processing expenses claims from social workers. Accounts have managed to manipulate the process such that the social workers spend longer than they should filling in the claim. This makes accounts efficient, but it takes the social workers away from spending time with clients. The overall system, which must be to provide support to the vulnerable in the community, has been sub-optimised. It would be in the interest of the whole system if accounts became less efficient and the social work system was therefore more effective.

The need for internal services should be pulled from core services. This means that when core services are designed, the function and design of support services like accounts, HR and IT should be subservient to service delivery.

More often than not, it is the other way round. We hear all the time of "IT led change". Such an approach is doing the wrong thing entirely. No doubt that IT can inform core services about what it is capable of so the service makes best use of the latest advances, but driving changes from a technology point of view is the best way to ensure a failed project. There are many examples in the public sector including the courts project, the NHS Connecting for Health and the Child Support Agency systems.

There is a similar story in HR. The type and rate of recruitment across departments in a local authority will vary enormously, but HR departments are notorious for applying the same processes to all departments. Of course, high standards should be expected from all departments, but high standards do not mean standardisation irrespective of recruitment needs.

Stakeholders

The problem of stakeholders is a more difficult one. There will be many parties that think they have a say or a stake in how an organisation or department operates. The key principle here is that by doing what is best for the customer, all the things that the stakeholders care about will come out right. It just takes some courage sometimes to stick to that principle.

In the end you need to ignore these stakeholders sometimes and carry on and do the right thing. At the same time you need to communicate with them fully so they can see that doing the right thing for customers in the long term sits well with whatever narrower interest they are nurturing.

Chapter 13

Flow versus scale

Economies due to scale are no myth, but flow gets the better result.

In manufacturing, economy due to scale translates into ever larger factories with bigger, faster machines that do only one thing very quickly. In service organisations this scale thinking actually leads to worse performance. In fact it does also in manufacturing. Toyota – in spite of their problems recently – have been world-beaters for decades by prioritising flow over scale.

Where does the belief in economy due to scale come from?

Mass production

Mass production was first realised in the industrial revolution when steam powered cotton and wool mills amplified the labour of the humans that ran the machines by many times. By attaching a power source you could run a machine much faster to produce cloth much more consistently and much more cheaply than having people sitting at looms doing it by hand.

In *The Wealth of Nations*,* Adam Smith wrote about pin making. He said that one man making the whole pin could possibly make 20 pins a day, but that in a team of pin-makers:

One man draws out the wire, another straights it, a third cuts it, a fourth points it, a fifth grinds it at the top for receiving the head; to make the head requires two or three distinct operations; to put it on, is a peculiar business, to whiten the pins is another; it is even a trade by itself to put them into the paper; and the important business of making a pin is, in this manner, divided into about eighteen distinct operations.

In this way a group of ten men can make 12 pounds of pins, which equates to about 4,800 pins a day each.

We can see why the division of labour was a popular method and with the addition of steam power was very successful.

The factory model was further enhanced when the Ford Motor Company invented the assembly line. This was a moving conveyor where a car moved slowly through the factory past the assembly points and was gradually put together as it travelled.

Massive stamping machines that could produce thousands of parts per day fed the assembly points.

Ford transformed the motorcar industry and took it from being craft work, with automobiles being made by a few men in a garage, to a modern industrial behemoth.

Are economies due to scale a myth?

Seddon† argues that economies of scale are a myth. We can safely say that this is an overstatement. Economies due to scale are not a myth.

---

*Smith, Adam. *The Wealth of Nations*, Penguin Classics; new edition (2003).

†http://www.thesystemsthinkingreview.co.uk/index.php?pg=18&backto=18&utwkst oryid=266&title=Why+do+we+believe+in+economy+of+scale%3F&ind=5

The trivial example of it being more economical to cook for two people than for one should put paid to that over simplification. The foreman in the pin factory that Adam Smith describes would have been seriously remiss not to do what he did when he increased productivity per worker from 20 pins to 4,800 pins per day.

To get over this assertion that economies of scale are a myth we need to look a little closer at what we mean when we use the word.

Scale as use of a common resource

Resource economies come when items are batched or processed en masse. So it is cheaper per part to fill a container with car parts and ship it around the world than it is to air freight each part individually. To take our cooking example it is more cost effective to prepare a large pan of Bolognese sauce for four than for one. The marginal costs for the heat to cook sauce for each person drops for each extra person. In education we can easily see the value of teaching in classes and having larger lecture halls at colleges and universities to impart knowledge and skills to many students at the same time. Public transport uses scale as bulk when we have trains and buses rather than people in cars. In office situations it is cheaper to have lots of people in a larger building rather than build a little hut for each of them. In each of these cases the reduction in space, rent, heating and lighting used per person means we can accommodate more students, patients and staff at a lower cost.

Scale as specialisation

This is the situation where it is better to have a person or piece of machinery concentrate on one narrow task. The Adam Smith pin story is an example of a string of specialisations by the workers in each stage of the pin making process.

In medicine it is not possible for someone to gain the sufficient skills, experience and knowledge to be effective in the every branch of medicine, so doctors who want to proceed to work as a consultant are forced to specialise.

Flow is more effective

However, just because we can see the efficacy of scale, it does not follow that it is the best or only way to increase productivity.

When Taiichi Ohno visited the USA in the 1950s he took most inspiration from seeing how people chose items from a supermarket shelf. He also visited car manufacturers and he saw the conveyor belts there. He grasped the concept of flow. He saw that the cars kept moving along the line. He saw the massive machines that served the parts and he asked, if flow seemed such a good idea for the main car, why was it not also best for all the other parts?

Ohno implemented what he saw as part of the Toyota Production System, a powerful combination of flow and pull.

Customers want personal service

Customers want a personal service. This is especially true for service organisations but is becoming more and more requested from manufacturing. People want to be treated differently wherever they spend their time or money. Some companies try to set up a Unique Selling Proposition by advertising a personal service. Do you recall the Burger King adverts with the slogan "Have it your way"?

Scale does not accommodate variety

In public services we have the analogous problem that people's circumstances and needs are different. So it is not so much that they are choosing to access different things but that we have to serve them. They are part of the service process and they are very different. We have to do a different job for every service user.

In fact, in manufacturing it looks like you can accommodate requests for variety and still keep economies due to scale as long as you run the big machines fast and fill warehouses with all the different possible requests that might come along. However, even in manufacturing they have realised that the money tied up in inventory held in expensive warehouses is a massive cost drain. They have come to the conclusion that making parts nearer to the time of request is more cost effective. Just-in-time production also has the added benefit of making quality problems easier to spot. If you are producing at the rate of demand, instead of filling half a warehouse with faulty parts, you can spot an error in an item sooner and rectify the problem before you have made too many more.

In service we don't have the option to pre-make parts since service is made at the point of interaction, so everything has to be done for each request. Unfortunately we still have the big factory mentality and we are constantly trying to replicate it even though our demand and work patterns mean it is not applicable.

There is still a desire to create local authority shared services where back office services such as HR and finance can be lumped together from neighbouring authorities. This is a factory scheme to try to create economies from scale.

Consequences of scale in service

When economies of scale are tried in service, performance deteriorates. The main reason is we try to replicate Adam Smith's pin factory and break work up into parts. Hence the work becomes fractured, the number of handovers increase, each worker becomes deskilled with respect to the process as a whole and flow suffers.

There is a penchant for front office/back office splits. We add a call centre peopled by staff who don't understand how the work is really processed to take calls, and a back office staff who can only talk to the customer via the front office. This means the flow of work is further broken. Because the call centre agents don't know the work, they often pass dirty information to the back office, which then has to be sorted out, leading to rework, errors and delay.

This model has been encouraged by central government.

Specialisation of skills

When we specialise skills, the work becomes repetitive and hence more boring. Staff become less flexible, which makes changing the work more difficult. The understanding of the system as a whole is lost to staff who are operating in an ever narrower sphere.

There is a risk that when we break up work into its parts we will start to optimise the parts to the detriment of the whole system, but also to the detriment of serving customers.

Batches

One of the aspects of economies of scale that disrupts the flow of work is that in order to maintain scale, work is bundled up into batches. That means that bunches of like work get done all together. This stops flow because every piece of work is waiting for every other piece of work to be done before the batch can move on. In service, people, and not massive machines, are doing this work, so the batches simply prevent work from moving smoothly on to the next step.

A good example of this is where hospitals are arranged around keeping the consultant doctors occupied. They batch patients by having weekly clinics that are for the same type of patient and then let patients sit in waiting rooms all day to be seen.

A member of my family had to have some polyps near his eyes removed. He was asked to attend the outpatient clinic at 8am. All day he waited and watched as the waiting room slowly emptied, until at 4pm he went in to have a procedure that lasted 20 minutes.

My grandfather recently had a cataract operation at the age of 93. It is brilliant that they offer that at his age, but it was not organised very well. He had to go in for an assessment appointment where they put drops in his eyes and then did various tests to see if he was suitable for the operation. In that assessment appointment he had to get up five times to see different nurses. Each nurse was doing one thing to a room full of elderly patients who were back and forth across the department all day. There was no reason why they could not have had each patient in at an appointed time and done all the tests together with the same nurse. Better still would be if my grandfather could have had the operation the same day after being assessed.

Principles of flow

As we have seen, the principles of flow are simple:

1. Get value to the customer as quickly as possible

2. Keep work moving

3. Every step adds value

4. Smaller batches are better – one-piece flow is best

Enhancing flow will cut costs. It will eliminate waiting lists and the cost of managing them. It will shorten the end-to-end time, which will eliminate the progress-chasing wasteful contacts. It will remove the batching and sorting. Errors can be corrected more quickly and thus have less impact on downstream process steps.

Flow vs. scale - conclusion

Economies due to scale are no myth, but especially in service, flow is the better place to start. This does not mean that we dismiss scale out of hand, rather that we need to be more careful and sophisticated in our use of scale versus flow. As a rule of thumb, when in doubt, promote flow. In the long run, there is a place for scale in most organisations; it just takes a more discerning eye to know when it is appropriate.

However, it is a tricky balancing act.

Take again the medical model. Above we bemoaned the model where the consultant is optimised to the detriment of the patient experience, but it is necessary that consultants must specialise since to have all of medical expertise in every doctor would be impossible. But simply because you have a valuable resource – a consultant doctor – it doesn't follow that this resource should be employed all the time. Don't assume that a valuable resource like a consultant is necessarily a bottleneck before you study your system.

More important is that the resource is ready to act when needed. That is seeing the doctor from the patient's point of view. "I am a patient, I have a need, is the doctor ready to see me as soon as is possible?" Rather than, "I am a doctor and a valuable resource and I should be made use of as much as is possible even if that inconveniences patients."

In the end, the choice between scale and flow is a false one. What we need to promote is the economy of a system optimised to deliver value to a customer. It has been recognised that the automatic application of scale is more often detrimental to the whole system than the promotion of end-to-end flow. However, in certain situations scale is a useful thing to have. You can only know which to use if you understand the underlying principles of each. Scale economy stems from the use of a common resource and flow economy comes from keeping value moving toward the customer. They both have their place and sometimes it is hard to see which is better. That is when you need to stop listening to the dogma about one or the other and run several experiments using HELP cycles to determine which is more beneficial to your system.

Chapter 14

Not all work is valid

Wasteful work should be eliminated. Working to correct something already done is clearly waste.

We can classify waste as everything that is not adding value, and we can reduce waste by eliminating these non-value adding steps and then having the value work flow.

What sort of waste is there in processes? Classically, Lean thinking defines seven wastes from manufacturing:

♦ **Overproduction – making more than is needed**

♦ **Waiting – work is not flowing**

♦ **Transportation – of the product**

♦ **Inventory – work in progress or parts waiting to be used**

♦ **Motion – excess movement of staff and equipment**

♦ **Over-processing – work that adds no value**

♦ **Rework – rectifying errors**

These wastes were developed for manufacturing so we have to use them with caution, but they can give us some clues to spotting waste in services. The two most relevant are waiting and rework. Waiting is normally caused by handovers and batching work, and rework is caused by dirty information at the start of the work and badly designed processes.

Can you think of examples of these wastes in your processes?

John Seddon describes other types of waste that are common in service. They are inspection, audit and verification.[*]

These arise from the tendency for government to want to specify work and then check that the organisation or staff are conforming to the specifications. This gives the wastes of:

♦ **Writing the specification**

♦ **Conforming to the specification**

♦ **Getting ready for the audit**

♦ **Conducting the audit**

When you have the situation where there are lots of targets, you also have processes that monitor and report on those targets. Given that targets are dysfunctional, all this monitoring work is therefore waste.

The typical waste steps are those that achieve absolutely nothing, like the sorting of the annual returns in a government department. In that case 3 of the 34 steps were found to add value. That is less than 10%. That means we can eliminate 90% of the steps in that process. We can combine this finding with the fact that 50% or more of contacts such as calls, letters, emails and visits from the public are usually wasteful contacts, to see the potential savings.

Let us visualise our service as we see it before we know these things:

---

[*]Seddon, John. *Systems Thinking in the Public Sector,* Triarchy Press (2008).

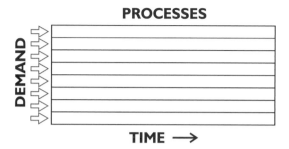

We then study our demand and find that half are wasteful contacts. So we shade those wasteful contacts and of course all the work to meet that demand is also therefore waste and we also shade it too.

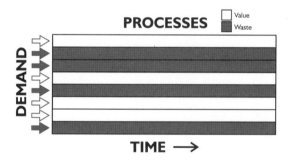

Having identified customer value, we now follow the process flows and find that only about 10% of the process steps are value, so we can shade all the waste.

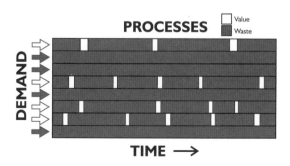

After removing the waste from the processes and designing out the causes of wasteful contacts we are left with this:

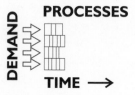

A tiny fraction of our work is value.

The required budget cuts don't seem so hard now and this is typical. We still have the same services but without the wasteful contacts and process waste they are drastically improved.

Chapter 15

Measures drive behaviour

People do what you measure. The measures in today's public sector are more suited to factories in the 19th century than to a modern service organisation.

The typical dysfunctional metrics are measuring busyness, efficiency and conformance to centrally set targets. However, none of these types of measures are good predictors of achievement or of good service to the public.

Measures of busyness

Busyness measures numerically track how fast an individual staff member or department is working but not whether they are being effective.

Number per period

The most common busyness measure is that of counting the number of pieces of work per set period, which is normally per day or per hour, e.g.

the number of claims per day or housing repairs per week or for data entry, keystrokes per hour.

Time to do

The most common time-to-do measure is Average Handle Time (AHT) in a call centre. This is an industry-wide measure in call centres, common in the public sector as well as the private sector. The handle time is the time from picking up the call to finishing any tasks to do with that call after putting the phone down. For example, a call may require a job to be raised in a customer relationship management (CRM) system after the call centre agent has put down the phone.

AHT is collated for individual agents, teams and the whole call centre. There is no doubt that it is an important measure for call centre planners since you need to know how many agents to employ to cope with the demand. But as a measure of individual performance, it is not very informative since it tells us nothing about how well the agent served the customer or whether that call should have been made in the first place.

We will see later how AHT distorts behaviour to the detriment of giving value to the public.

Time elapsed

While time elapsed in some cases is an appropriate measure, it is only right if it is of value to a service user, and it covers the whole end-to-end time of the delivery of a service from initiation to final finishing. The problem comes when time elapsed is applied to parts of a service such that small sections of a process are optimised to reduce elapsed time while worsening the service as a whole.

Ambulance services are targeted on three different types of calls. The most important is category A – emergency calls – e.g. suspected heart attacks. These must be responded to within 8 minutes for 75% of these calls.

The targets are the same across the country. Clearly it is difficult to provide the same service in rural Wales as in metropolitan Manchester since the reasons for calls, the volumes, distances, traffic and many other variables are different. There is an open question about whether we should expect exactly the same service all over the country or if the service should meet the varying demand.

Accident and Emergency departments had a target to deal with arriving patients within four hours. This led to some A&E departments admitting patients to wards when it was not necessary. This blocked beds for those who really needed them and spread patients around the hospital, with surgery patients in medical wards simply so they could get them out of A&E to stop the department breaching the target.

The problem with simple averages

Averages such as the AHT measure in call centres have further problems. By simply using an average you lose information about the spread of the call times. You can have two sets of calls that all have an AHT of 5 minutes, but the first cluster closely around 5 minutes and the second set varies wildly from a few seconds to 10 minutes. The two sets of calls have the same AHT but have very different characteristics. Chapter 4 on understanding variation described how to deal with this in more detail.

Measures skew behaviour

We have already seen that Accident and Emergency departments in the NHS have changed their behaviour to meet the measures and targets. This behaviour is to be expected when you are measured, rated and rewarded on the basis of hitting these targets and measures.

Call centre agents would not be human if they didn't cheat to get their AHT down. Time is money and less time on the phone means more time to take another call. Call centres that get paid by the call want more calls hence a lower AHT.

Agents will resort to putting the phone down on difficult callers, forwarding calls to inappropriate departments and fobbing callers off to get onto the next call.

If 75% of category A ambulance calls need to be seen in 8 minutes, what do you suppose happens to the other 25%? When a category A call is clearly not going to be seen inside the target, do they just let it ride since 8 minutes and 1 second is just as bad as 20 minutes?

When this happens, the behaviour of the organisation is in turn skewed since managers no longer trust agents, the Department of Health no longer trusts A&E departments or ambulance services and a whole set of checks, audits and inspections is thought to be needed to keep people on the straight and narrow.

Kashmir soldiers

The worst example I have come across is where the police in Kashmir, on the border of India and Pakistan, are investigating Indian soldiers because they believe that the soldiers are killing civilians and pretending that the bodies are those of Muslim terrorists.[*] The Indian soldiers are reported to be targeted on how many Islamic terrorists they kill.

How far could measures of busyness take you?

Hit the target, miss the point

The common thread here is that we are hitting the target, optimising the measure, but missing the point. Accident and Emergency departments are there to treat patients, not hit targets. Call centre agents are there to give a service to callers, not reduce their average handle time.

The irony is that when measures of busyness and targets relating to them are dropped, not only does the public get a better service but those measures also improve.

Take the example of a call to notify a council of a change of address. If the agent takes the time to ensure that the address has been properly

---

[*]http://www.guardian.co.uk/world/2010/jun/29/kashmir-deaths-indian-soldiers-investigated

recorded it will take longer than if she rushes it, and that will push up her AHT. However, if she rushes the call and gets the new address wrong then the wasteful contacts into the council call centre in the coming months will be manifold. The caller could be missing council tax bills, be paying the wrong rate, potentially be missing benefits notifications, etc. The caller will have to call the council to get all of these resulting mistakes rectified. A few seconds extra on the original call will save hours of calls over the next year.

A friend has the first name Rajendra. Here we will change his surname to Prasad. He has grown used to having to spell out his first name over the phone. In this story he was on the phone to a call centre and was asked his name. He replied, "Rajendra. That's 'R' for Romeo..." at that point he was interrupted by the agent asking for his surname. He assumed that this time the agent had heard and understood his first name correctly. However, it wasn't too long before he received a letter from the company addressed to an "Arthur Romeo Prasad".

Monitoring breeds resentment

People like to be trusted and they respond well to it. If you want staff to act responsibly, then give them responsibility. Many organisations do the exact opposite. They don't trust their staff and they treat them like children or criminals. This may sound like a harsh description, but there are many examples of condescending management techniques that are based on the flawed assumption that people are lazy cheats.

Timed toilet breaks

It is not uncommon in call centres for staff to have their toilet breaks timed. This is done via an availability measure. The IT system tracks how available an agent is to take the next call. The agents can flag themselves as having a toilet break, which is logged on the system. There are stories of some places putting a maximum time on such breaks. Do the management in these call centres wonder why call centres have such a high turnover of staff?

Average handle time prevents good work

The tyranny of the average handle time (AHT) measure prevents agents in call centres from dealing with calls properly. The supervisors are constantly pushing agents to deal with calls faster and to stick to set scripts. But the most pernicious problem is that this pushing for quicker calls and hence worse customer service is undermining the agent's self-esteem. People want to do a good job, and even though a call centre agent isn't the most prestigious job out there, once in the job, people want to do it as well as they can. By putting in place pressures from AHT and the limitations of scripts, agents are prevented from doing the best work they can.

Some call centre agents work around the system to help when they shouldn't. When I was moving out of a flat last year, the agent in the council call centre said that my council tax direct debit should sort itself out but that it usually doesn't, so I should cancel it with my bank at my end so no extra payments are taken. He said, "Otherwise it will take months to get the money back."

Why do good people need to circumvent the system? Because otherwise the system would prevent them from doing their jobs properly. However, if caught, agents would be in trouble for straying from the procedures; procedures they know produce wasteful contacts. This is the responsibility of management, but it can only properly be remedied by management and staff working together.

One job for tradesmen

A council officer in the North East told me that previously they would give batches of jobs to tradesmen that carried out repairs to the council housing stock. So a carpenter might get four or five jobs for that day. They were finding that they couldn't trust the tradesmen to do the jobs in the order on the sheet, so they had instituted mobile technology. Now when the tradesmen tell control that they have finished their current job, they are issued the next job. By changing from a batch of jobs to one at a time, the local authority has reduced its trust in the tradesmen.

I would wager that those tradesmen were adjusting the order of the jobs to make best use of time. Getting one job at a time will be sending them hither and thither with no way to prepare or optimise their route for that day.

In fact, the better solution would be for the tradesmen to have geographical areas that they have responsibility for. They could also have responsibility for dealing with tenants directly to arrange and perform maintenance and repairs. The details of the system would be worked out by managers and tradesmen in tandem and would be designed to optimise the service to the tenants.

This is a strange idea to some people. When I suggested such a possible plan to the officer in question, he looked at me as if I were a little odd. I must have seemed even more odd, given the expression on his face, when I suggested trusting the tradesmen with organising their own work.

Trust is returned

When people are trusted they are happier in their work, they trust their managers proportionately and they are more willing to go the extra mile. Whereas in the old system going the extra mile meant getting around the system to serve the customer, in the new system it means working to improve the system so they never have to work around the work to serve the customer.

An area of responsibility

You can give responsibility in many different ways. Staff can be given dominion over a section of the work or customers, for example a type of customer like children or those with learning disabilities or larger planning applications.

The responsibility might be geographical. This will suit road or housing repairs. Staff become proud of keeping their patch well run.

They might be given a speciality, such as social workers who work specifically with drug users or educational welfare officers who work solely with migrant families.

Measure value for the customer

The core idea is to identify value for the customer and then design the system of work to deliver that value. We need, therefore, to measure the value that the customer specifies. It is important to clearly state here that we mean value as defined by the customer, not by any internal, management or other external influences. It is only by defining and measuring true customer value that the real benefits are realised.

Get quick feedback

Your customers will already be giving feedback on what they value. Every time they contact you to chase progress or complain of a missed dustbin or an error on their account, they are giving you information on what is valuable to them.

It is interesting to note that if your service is particularly poor at the moment, then customers may have already lowered their expectations. Just because they call after a few weeks to find out about their benefits rather than a few days, it doesn't mean that they are happy to get their money at that time. As soon as possible is better in that case.

More satisfying work

Directly measuring what is valuable is better for staff since they can see that a change in that measure will reflect a change for the better for the public they serve. They will currently be trying to optimise management or regulatory measures that mean nothing to them. Customer related measures that improve due to the efforts of staff produce much more satisfaction.

What do customers value?

The most common measure is end-to-end time. Many things fall into this. Benefits are a good example. Any service where sooner is better will use this as a direct measure of customer value. Other examples are planning applications, treatment in the NHS and response times to street crime by the police.

Seeing no problems is the next most common measure. Potholes are a funny thing since actually the time to fix a pothole is not the main thing. The thing of most value is that there are no potholes in the first place. That is down to well-maintained roads. The end-to-end time of each maintenance job is important, but people prefer a little bother from an effective maintenance programme to the greater inconvenience of potholes appearing in their roads.

I used to live on a road in London where they never fixed the potholes properly. They would come and patch them every now and then. I would have preferred that they shut the road for two days to properly resurface. Instead, for nearly five years, they came back every three months to patch the constantly recurring holes in the road.

Convenience is the next measure. Sometimes speed is not the most important thing. If you have a dripping tap and you are going out that afternoon, being told that you have to stay in so a plumber can call is annoying, even if it is fast. Perhaps a week next Wednesday is more convenient.

Chapter 16

Behavioural pressures

The silent causes of a dysfunctional system must be removed.

What are behavioural pressures?

In every work system there are policies and procedures that prevent change and innovation. Examples are targets, pay structures, bonuses, inspection policies and departmental organisation.

These behavioural pressures are embedded into the system and thus are harder to see than most of the things that cause waste like non-value process steps or wasteful contacts.

Some of the behavioural pressures will come up in the process mapping where you follow work from end to end. There will be policies and incentives that will cause the problems you find in the process. Ensure that you note these down.

Behavioural pressures are the reasons why our system is like it is. System level behavioural pressures are the things that change our behaviours. We have seen that targets and pay change behaviour and also that inspection will cause error rates to go up. Anything that causes a system to be the way it is or that changes the way we react or see the work is a behavioural pressure.

Examples of behavioural pressures

Internal pressures

- ♦ **Policy decisions**
- ♦ **Internal targets**
- ♦ **Pay/bonuses**
- ♦ **Goals**
- ♦ **Coaching**

External pressures

- ♦ **External targets**
- ♦ **Regulation**
- ♦ **Audit**

Structural pressures

- ♦ **Hierarchy**
- ♦ **Team formation**
- ♦ **Management style**

Can't avoid policies altogether

You can't get away from having a pay structure or policies, but you can remove the things that are dysfunctional.

Policies and systems should be simple

Systems should be as simple as possible to achieve their reason. This means aligning departments with the flow of work, and removing complex pay and bonus structures that cause attention to be taken away from the work. Policies should be constructive but minimal.

When a large media company implemented a new company intranet system they scrapped the thousands of words that tried to tell users of the old system how to interact and treat each other properly. Instead they replaced the pages of policy with the single sentence, "Don't be a dick".

In short, remove those behavioural pressures you can and simplify the rest.

Management support

In order to remove these behavioural pressures you will need upper management support since the behavioural pressures will have been around for a while. You need to present evidence of the effect that these policies and incentives are having. You also need a credible argument as to why removing them will improve things. Of course if you can get upper management closely involved in the improvement work, studying demand and processes, this becomes much easier.

Finance is a behavioural pressure

Finance and departmental budgets can be highly dysfunctional. Managers are always fighting for budget and headcount since that is the way they get prestige. Budgets are fought for whether or not they are needed. The fight takes place on a just-in-case basis and then money is spent even though there should be an underspend in a function in a year.

I recall doing some casual work at a local secondary school installing computers in classrooms. As the time went on I discovered that there were hundreds of computers hidden in cupboards all over the school. They were at least three years old, some more than five, and had been bought with excess budget in previous years. Given the speed with which computer equipment dates they were all virtually useless by the time I found them. "We had to spend our budget," sighed the head of IT when I asked him about it. The same school had offered three years' fees up front to a computer contractor to clear the IT budget for that year.

Where possible, budgets should be made fungible across the organisation. This means that where money needs to be spent in one department to make a greater saving in another department, the barriers to moving that money need to be removed.

New accounting

The accounting and finance of public sector bodies is very strict. This is to be expected since we are dealing with taxpayers' money. However, a new way of allocating budgets needs to be found. As well as being able to move money between departments, the way budgets are allocated over financial years is just as important. Christian Wolmar writes in *Down the Tube** that on average the London Underground has had enough money over the last 40 years to keep up a good maintenance schedule on the network. However, the amount of money has varied so much from year to year that planning a consistent schedule was impossible. One year there would be too much money and so for fear of losing it they would spend on things that they either knew were not needed or knew they couldn't finish. Then in the tight years they had to skimp on work they knew really needed doing.

Talking to an officer in a London borough, he told me that he and his peers would underspend in the first half of most financial years in case cuts were announced part way through the year. Then they would overspend to make up the surplus carried from the first part of the year to ensure they spent the budget so they got the same amount the next financial year.

This hoarding then splurging of funds is not isolated to the public sector – I saw it when I used to work in investment banks – but it means that there are underfunded services, followed by money lashed out on spurious projects in the latter part of the year. This is a big waste.

A new way of managing budgets needs to be found, not specifically to prevent this behaviour, since that sounds like more audit, monitoring and blame, but rather to let managers and staff know that achieving the reason is the primary aim and that they should try to pull funds, as they would any other resource, when needed.

---

*Wolmar, Christian. *Down The Tube: The Battle for London's Underground*, Aurum Press (2002).

Chapter 17

Transactional services

A request is made,

work is done,

value is delivered.

Simple but not simplistic

We start with the simple case first, that of simple, linear, transactional systems. These are systems where the value delivered is simple to identify and the reason easy to express. Systems where the work follows a linear process, one step followed by another. The interaction between the customer and the organisation is that of a transaction.

A transaction is where the customer makes a request, work is done and value is delivered.

Commercial transactions

An obvious example is a sale. A customer wants a chocolate bar or a new van, they choose the one they want, pay the money and off they go with their new purchase.

That description of a sale belies the thousands or perhaps millions of tasks that need to be completed to get that chocolate bar or van into the hands of the customer. But there is a linear progression that produces, ships and sells these products. It is linear in the sense that a river is linear. There maybe many creeks and streams that eventually feed into the main river in the same way that the cocoa beans and the chocolate bar packaging come from different places to be combined into the final product. There is no single line to be traced from the customer to the origin of the process, but like a river there are many lines that can be traced back to their respective sources. The additive effect of those sources running together and gaining power along the way is what gives us the high-value goods we enjoy.

Although these systems are simple and linear it is evident that they are not simplistic. Many of the steps that comprise the processes that come together are, when taken alone, very complicated. They may require great knowledge or skill and have been perfected over many years. It is still the case that linear analytical methods such as process mapping are extremely useful in improving these processes that eventually deliver value.

Transactional request

It is the nature of the request that is the sharpest pointer to whether a system is transactional or complex. As we shall see in the next section, complex systems can be characterised by a relationship between the customer and the organisation. In a transactional system there is the minimum possible relationship between the customer and the organisation. In order for me to buy the chocolate bar, or the van for that matter, the seller does not need to get to know me as a person at all. I may have to prove that I am capable of payment or that I have the right permissions to purchase the goods in question, but apart from very simple criteria, a transaction requires no personal knowledge of the customer to proceed.

As an aside, it is interesting to note that more and more, transactional organisations are trying to strike up a relationship with customer so that they can 1) give them better, more personalised service, 2) better target their marketing, and 3) try to inspire loyalty in customers.

Transactions in public services

So far we have been talking about chocolate and vans. This is clearly in the commercial sector. So are there any simple, linear, transactional services in the public sector? There are a few that are genuinely transactional and many more that look transactional but are not.

A good example of a transactional service is household refuse collection. As a householder, my request is that my rubbish and recycling are collected. The terms are that I must pay my council tax and present the rubbish in the appropriate bag or bin, in the time and place as told to me by my local council. In return the council will regularly remove my rubbish and recycling and dispose of it accordingly.

There is no personal relationship in refuse collection and disposal. Neither the council nor the bin men need to know me in order to best collect my rubbish. The request is clear and the result required is easy to explain.

Housing benefit taken by itself is another example of a transaction. A person who thinks they may be entitled to housing benefits presents their circumstances to the council. The council goes away and assesses their entitlement, says no or yes, and if yes, how much. They then proceed to set up payment. The fact that the claimant is providing personal details does not mean that there is a personal relationship between them and the council or even between the claimant and the officer assessing the claim.

In benefit claims the work is linear, the request simple and the relationship transactional.

However, we shall see in the next section that while a request seen on its own may be transactional, just like a benefits claim, when a service user has to engage in many of these transactions they become the centre of a complex human system.

Improving transactional systems

In deriving a method to improve simple, linear, transactional systems we can build on the work of John Seddon and the Vanguard Model for Check.* The rest of the section uses this as a basis with some amendments that have come from practical experience.

Demand in transactional services

It is obvious that matching capacity to demand means that you are neither wasting resources with extra capacity nor are you unable to meet demand with a lack of capacity. Unfortunately this is often as far as the analysis of demand goes in most organisations.

Organisations don't understand demand

Don't think it is important

Measuring demand against capacity is seen as enough by organisations since we are here to do the work that comes in. Hence we need just the right amount of resource to cope with that demand. Organisations don't take the time to ask further questions about their demand.

Don't measure demand

Many organisations never seem to ask these elementary questions:

♦ **Who is placing the demand?**

♦ **What different demands are coming in?**

♦ **When is demand arriving?**

♦ **What type of demand is it? – Wanted or wasteful?**

♦ **Is demand predictable?**

---

*Chapter 6 of Seddon, John. *Freedom from Command and Control,* Triarchy Press (2005)

Organisations are defined from the outside

Demand is essential to understand since the types of demand that you get define a transactional service. You might think that you define your service from the inside, but this is not so.

In the coming years the NHS will have to provide more and more care for elderly patients as we all live longer. There will be more old people who spend a larger part of their lives suffering from the types of ailments that the young rarely get such as osteoporosis and dementia. The NHS has no choice but to serve this demand and as such is defined from the outside.

What you offer customers is who you think you are

Your offer to customers is who you think you are. You define your service and then hope to meet those promises.

What you do for customers is who you actually are. If you are full of waste, delay and error then that is your service, not what you promised.

So your service is defined from the outside, but the quality of service is defined by what you do, not what you say.

Is demand predictable?

Most managers will tell you that their demand is unpredictable. This means they don't think that they can say how much demand they will get in the next hour, tomorrow, next week or next month. Actually I have not come across a service where demand is not predictable. That is not to say that you can tell exactly how many planning applications will arrive in the next month, but you should be able to say within limits what your minimum and maximum expected demand will be. This is to do with an understanding of variation, which we dealt with more fully in Chapter 4.

You may have to take into account seasonal or periodic cycles to see the stable processes. For example, people often ring complaints departments on a Monday since they have been meaning to do it all weekend and there are the obvious examples of holidays and seasons that affect some services.

Once it is determined that demand is predictable, we can begin to study the types of demand.

Type of demand

The next error is treating all demand as if it were valid. A local authority should be happy to get the call to be notified of a resident's change of address. They should not be happy to receive a call of complaint or progress chasing. That is extra work that is wasting money.

Wanted contacts

Wanted contacts are requests, in their various forms – telephone calls, emails, personal visits, etc. – that the customer is happy to make. In the private sector we say they are happy to pay for it. You can also think of it as the customer being happy to participate.

For example, a resident is fine about making the change of address call.

Wanted contacts are about what the organisation is here to do – we come back to the reason. If the contact goes along with the reason it is most probably a wanted contact.

Wasteful contacts

Wasteful contacts[*] are contacts that are caused by the organisation making an error or not doing something it should have done.

When the resident calls back to say that council correspondence is still going to her old address, this is the result of not doing something. If she were to call to say that the new address is wrong, that is an error.

Some more examples of wasteful contacts:

---

[*]This is from the idea of "failure demand" from John Seddon, see *Freedom for Command and Control* (2005)

- ◆ A call to say that a payment for council tax has not been credited against the account.

- ◆ A surgery patient has to have another operation to remove a piece of surgical equipment that was left inside them during the first operation.

- ◆ A call because a claimant doesn't understand the questions on the form.

- ◆ A social worker is not allocated in a timely manner and the situation deteriorates before any assessment can be made.

- ◆ An elderly person's request for simple home changes such as handrails on the stairs is not met. The person has a fall and ends up in hospital with a fracture.

- ◆ Housing benefit entitlement is delayed causing a tenant to miss rent payments that end up with eviction proceedings and a court case.

We can see with the last two examples that wasteful contacts can cross service boundaries. The failure of adult social care to meet the basic home needs of the elderly person led to a major demand on the NHS. Similarly the housing benefit office causes wasteful contact for the landlord and the courts.

The effect of wasteful contacts on the public should not be underestimated. While vulnerable people are trying to access services that might help their situation, having set backs, errors and delays to benefits and other assistance might be consuming time that they could be using more productively. Not to mention the stress, worry and family problems that can result.

Improvement steps for transactional services

Evaluate contacts

First we need to examine all the requests coming in to see whether they are wanted or wasteful contacts. Depending on your systems, this can be a fairly manual process of going back through logs. It may mean days of sitting listening to calls. Sometimes this is actually the best way since call centre agents can mistake wanted for wasteful contacts quite easily if you let them record it themselves.

It can be instructive to listen to the words that callers use at the start of a call.

Classify all the requests into wanted and wasteful but also group them into common themes, e.g. for wanted it might be: new claim, change of address and change of financial circumstances; for wasteful it might be: progress chasing, incorrect amount of money, appealing entitlement, money not received, etc.

These groups should be assigned a frequency so we can see which is the most common.

Identify value

The key is to identify the value to the customer and to keep that uppermost in your mind.

Eliminate wasteful contacts quickly

If there are short-term changes that can be made to remove wasteful contacts then do them using the HELP method to guide you.

Wanted contacts drive design

When redesigning work, you must design against your reason. What do we mean by this? It means that we design the work to meet the wanted contacts. We don't design in ways to cope with any wasteful contacts. That will be designed out.

When you put together the new processes and workflows you are doing it to make the value work flow with no errors, delays or rework. The new processes will complete work quickly and get it right the first time. In this way wasteful contacts will be eliminated at source.

What you must not do is design new processes that constantly check for errors. Do not have processes with lots of inspection for example. Inspection will cause error rates to go up since you are removing responsibility from the person who does the work. The person who does the work will expect the inspector to pick up any errors and the inspector will expect the original work to have been done right most of the time so won't inspect as closely as you might think. Error rates go down when you eliminate inspection and make the person responsible for the work. This doesn't mean a dressing down whenever there is an error, the opposite in fact. This means the person is responsible for how the work is done and how it is changed to eliminate the possibility of error.

Organisations put in whole departments to deal with wasteful contacts. Complaints departments are the best example. They are a department dedicated to dealing with errors, waste and unhappy customers. Your goal is to design them out of existence.

My first job at Chase Manhattan Bank was in the Middle Office of the Interest Rate Group. The job of the Middle Office was to reconcile the profit and loss that the traders reported against the profit and loss that the back office systems reported. If they didn't match, we had to find the reason – a wrongly entered trade, a trade not entered at all, a trader's incorrect spread sheet model, a wrong swap curve for that product, etc. The whole department was about inspection and rectifying errors. We didn't spend much time, if any at all, on helping the traders, trade input or the back office to avoid the errors in the first place, so the same errors came along every day and we mopped them up. This is an organisational design to encourage waste.

Section 4

Complex Human
Services

Chapter 18

Beyond transactions

Organisations deliver value
in many different ways.
Understanding value can change
the way it is delivered.

Shape of value

The way that value is delivered by organisations can vary enormously. Some deliver value in one-off transactions, some by maintaining infrastructure and others in longer-term relationships with customers. The way that organisations view their current shape of value delivery will influence the way they design services. It is also the case that an organisation can get locked into seeing themselves as delivering services in a particular way when it may be that a different model will serve the customer better and achieve the purpose more effectively.

The method of demand analysis described at the end of the previous section is useful insofar that demand is transactional. This means that there is a clear boundary between the organisation and the user of the service. It usually means that the work to provide the service, once it has been requested, does not involve the user in the delivery. As discussed, the simplest transaction is a purchase. A customer goes to a bookshop, selects the book they wish to buy, pays for it and leaves. The provision of the value – the writing, production, storage, shipping and display of the book – requires no interaction from the book buyer. A bookseller may adjust the books held, the design, the layout or the location of the bookshop to increase sales, but the provision of value has a clear boundary.

In complex public services this clear boundary is rapidly becoming blurred. Not only is the service user often intimately involved at the point of delivery of value, they are often instrumental in achieving the desired outcome.

We can think of examples like surgery where obviously the patient is required to be present to complete the procedure. But it is also the case that swift, effective recovery from many procedures requires the patient to do daily exercise, take further medication and attend outpatient appointments. Not to forget the need to adhere to procedures before attending the hospital for example going nil by mouth in the hours before their appointment. The patient is now a part of the system. We can even go so far as to say that they are one of the many parts that need to function in order to have a successful outcome. This will become more common as medical procedures become more complex and involved.

Staying in the medical arena, this idea of the patient being inside the system, rather than outside can already be seen in the treatment of chronic conditions. Further, it is more common now for patients to take equipment home to be able to self-monitor. The number of kidney patients who are seeing the benefits of home dialysis is on the increase. The same is true of the self-monitoring of patients with COPD who may now have devices in their home to take tests that get reported to a specialist nurse back at the hospital trust without the patient attending an appointment at all.

While the surgery example shows that the patient starts to be inside the system, the home procedure examples show that patients are taking what was before considered part of the system (expensive medical equipment) home with them. They are widening the location of components of the system beyond the traditional boundaries.

In adult social care the emphasis on caring for the elderly at home rather than admitting them to homes is another example. But we can also see that services such as drug and alcohol support are dependent on the user to do the bulk of the work to remedy the situation. Support workers can only provide help; it is the service user who has to put what they learn into action. The active member in delivering the value is no longer the employee of the council or hospital trust. The operative person is the user themselves.

These types of support services also point up another interesting twist where the service users get value from other service users in the form of support groups. Groups to help stop smoking give the attendees value from the other attendees. A professional will be there to facilitate but the value comes from the other members of the group sharing their trials and successes.

So we can see that while the "inside out" view is certainly discredited, looking "outside in" while better, is not sufficient to explain the interaction of users with modern services.

We have looked at services where the request is simple, the work is linear and the demand is transactional. These services can be dealt with by first studying demand. For these services the value is in the work and so to identify value we follow the work.

It is important to understand the small number of cases where simple, linear, transactional services can be improved, since it is a base to build upon when we come to improve more complicated services.

The problem comes when we realise that the majority of public services are not transactional.

Public services are not transactional

We could just stop with the assumption that all public services are transactional. For example, we could assume that children's services are transactional. This is to say, if we take this at face value, we would believe that children's services could be improved by treating all the contacts between the child and their family and the various agencies as singular transactions. Then if we dealt with each of these transactions and classified them each as value contacts or wasteful contacts and worked to increase the value contacts satisfied in a timely manner and at the same time to reduce or eliminate wasteful contacts, then we will make children's services better and cut costs.

However, this would be a gross simplification of a complex service. It ignores the subtlety of the understanding of human relationships in such cases. It skirts over the complexity of the communications between the various agencies involved in child protection or similar situations. The co-ordination problem faced when you have the input of social workers, police, teachers, educational welfare officers, GPs, hospital consultants and others all interacting with many contacts, opinions and recommendations, is significant. It is not a problem that will yield simply to making each contact more efficient in a transactional sense.

Children's services are a very human problem. It is the time taken to understand the situation of a child or a child, its siblings, parents or carers and wider family and friends that brings results. That depth of insight cannot be gleaned from a series of transactions.

Similarly a social worker will need to be more than familiar with the lives of a whole family in order to help them with what can be lifelong issues. A superficial contact with a client will not bring the individual understanding and help required. It makes it all the sadder that many parts of the country suffer from a high turnover of social work staff. In these areas you can't the blame the staff as individuals for the situation, but from the point of view of their clients, they see a revolving gallery of social workers sometimes month to month, which does nothing to help them to get a handle on their problems.

A primary school teacher would be considered pretty poor if she took no effort to get to know the children in her class. In order to produce lively, interested, confident and educated pupils a teacher will have to make efforts to get to know them as individuals, to find out their interests and learning styles.

Other examples are adult social care and treating patients with chronic conditions. However, there are many services that on the face of them may seem transactional, but treating them as such would be dysfunctional. For example, a planning application may look like a transaction, but the consequences of giving or withholding permission to build, alter a property or to change use is not confined to that application or property. The decision affects the environment of whole communities. Some decisions are large and obvious, but the cumulative effect of many small decisions can drastically change an area in a short period of time.

That said I am certainly not advocating dropping the analysis of demand entirely, far from it. It is a useful technique in the right situation. It is simply that if we believe W. Edwards Deming was correct when he said we shouldn't copy, then neither should we necessarily start by studying demand in all services.

Public services are complex and complicated

Public services are complicated. They are messy and difficult to get your head around. This is partly to do with the waste that they contain, but it is also because all the parts are connected to a multitude of other parts. The education system does not just influence the exam results of students it also affects crime, social cohesion, jobs, business, research, family life and many other areas. So to say that we can measure education excellence simply by counting exam grades is folly.

This complication makes public services difficult to understand and therefore difficult to improve. It also makes improvement efforts hard to start let alone complete. Knowing where to begin is tough and simplistic prescriptions abound concerning what to do first.

Complex versus complicated

It is worth making a distinction between complex and complicated. A complex is a structure or system that is made up of many simple parts. Think of a house made of Lego bricks. While the house has the trait of being a house that is greater than the sum of its parts, the bricks, it is still only made up of simple plastic bricks. To design the house is still a subtle problem, but to put it together given the bricks and clear instructions is literally child's play.

Something that is complicated, like the human brain, is usually something that we don't yet fully understand, or that we could not recreate. The human brain is also a complex, being made up of simple cells such as synapses and neurons, but it has the added complication of exhibiting emotion, reason, morality and other human traits that we cannot yet fully explain.

Public services are partially amenable to analysis to reveal their complex nature – being made up of simple parts – but they are still complicated. This means that they are still hard to understand and difficult to improve.

When faced with complex problems we can use analysis to break them down into their constituent simple parts. With complicated problems we need some other method of insight until either we solve the problem or we reduce the problem to one that is complex. For example, as we gain greater knowledge about the brain, it will slowly reduce from a complicated problem to a complex problem.

The key to be able to understand and improve public services is to identify the insight that will unlock the problem. For transactional services, the key is demand. For complex human services like child protection, we need something else. But first we need to be able to distinguish between simple, linear, transactional services and complex human services.

Identifying complex human services

The simple classification of a complex human service is one that is too complicated to improve by using transactional methods alone. But we can provide some pointers that a service is more complicated than a transactional one with the following observations.

Multiple transactions

Where individual parts of a service are transactional but as a whole the service is made up of many transactions it is common that the interactions of those transactions are complex. This is also true if this is the case when we take the view of the customer.

A GP surgery could be viewed as a collection of transactions. Patients book and attend a series of appointments with doctors, nurses and other professionals to receive advice, treatment, prescriptions and referrals to other medical services. Each one is a transaction, but taken as a whole it is a complex system where transactions influence each other. If you arrive to find that the nurse knows nothing of the last appointment with your doctor you have to spend time explaining why you were referred to the nurse which then leaves less time for your treatment. Patients would agree that a continuous relationship with a particular doctor who knows you and your family, is much more effective and reassuring than seeing a different doctor every visit and relying on the medical notes to communicate your history to the next new doctor for each appointment.

Ongoing

In an ongoing service such as in mental health. Patients may be in the system for many years and in contact with many different agencies and professions at different times of their lives as their condition and lives change. Considering each of these contacts as a transaction only scratches the surface of the need of such patients.

Multiple agency

Just like mental health there are many services such as social services that require the intervention of many agencies working together. This problem of integration and co-ordination is not linear, simple or transactional.

Require relationships

Where a service requires a relationship with a service user in order to be successful, the transactional model also comes up short. Take addiction services. To help an alcoholic or drug addict get the help they need takes an understanding of their personal life, circumstances, family, friends and work. In addition these types of services require the co-operation and participation of the service user to be successful. A recovering alcoholic will have to do much of the work themselves to improve their life. This will be with the support of professionals who know them personally and can give them tailored advice.

Projects

Project work is complex and complicated. There is no series of demands from which we can discern the value and waste contacts. A project can be set up to last for years and involve many hundreds of people. Often the success or otherwise is only known as the project comes close to being finished.

In projects, the use of resources and the definition of the purpose of the project is the key to eliminating waste and producing a valuable output. The field of project management is beyond the scope of this book. Suffice it to say that the advice is to keep it simple. Try not to get sucked into the vortex of Gantt charts, progress meetings and project managers that don't understand the domain.

No direct request

There are needs in the community that don't display easily identifiable demand patterns. The setting up of Sure Start centres to support pre-school children and their parents did not come from people calling or visiting their local council. It came because a need was identified that certain families would benefit from extra support, advice and skills early on in a child's life to boost that child's life prospects and make parents more confident in their parenting skills. If we had waited for demand to unearth this need, Sure Start would never have been initiated.

These type of needs can come from family or friends for individuals where the person themselves doesn't realise their need for a service. A nurse might ask whether a patient is receiving the benefits to which the patient might be entitled. The police may refer someone to mental health services on the advice of a duty psychiatrist.

Internal support services

Talking about transactions, relationships and projects often gets blank look from a large body of staff in the public sector. These are the internal support services like HR, IT and legal to name but a few. These organisations don't interact directly with the public but at the same time they are essential to service delivery. A lot of them are incredulous when they hear that front line services are to be protected at their expense since they know that what they provide is indispensible. The staff on the front line will often agree with that since when support services are cut it is often the case that front line staff are expected to do the work themselves. The police are expecting that cuts in civilian staff will mean more paperwork for officers, which takes officers away from the public. All in the name of protecting front line policing. Note that the problem here is not the officers versus the civilian staff, it is whether, whoever has to do it, the paperwork actually adds any benefit to the service to the public.

With internal support services, the key is to see them as another layer of the front line work. In order to provide true value to front line staff, support services need to truly understand the value that the front line is providing so it can dove-tail into that delivery. It has already been stated that the view of the internal customer is a red herring, but it is also dysfunctional. It leads to support services being viewed as cost centres trying to make "profits" from the way they serve other parts of the organisation. If we are fighting amongst ourselves for budget and prestige, what chance does the public have of ever receiving even an adequate service?

When internal support services decide to see the external customer they do not only assist front line staff but they can also see opportunities to do things that the front line staff without specialist knowledge will not even know is possible. For example, working on the road with laptops and other mobile devices is something that front line and IT staff can perfect together to give a better service to the public. Alone, they would not have the combined skill set to make the most of it. The front line staff would not have the complete knowledge of the possibilities of the technology and the IT department would not be able to see the most optimal use to which new technologies can be put. These collaborations must always have the service user as the priority. Overuse of inappropriate technology is always a risk when its use is seen as an end in itself.

Shape shifting

The type of delivery can change. Sometimes that change will be because of new technology, or from government policy and sometimes from pressure of public opinion. The most useful situation is when a service re-evaluates how it sees itself.

For example, most highways departments are years behind the pothole repairs in their area. They struggle to keep up with the number of potholes that get reported. On top of the normal wear and tear of the roads, every winter the roads deteriorate badly. This cycle of chasing repairs is not very productive. The department sees itself as reactive. It responds to repairs that need to be done as fast as it can. The solutions that are sought are to make the department more efficient at effecting repairs. These solutions can be very effective at boosting the productivity of repairs. However, the shape of the department is still reactive and transactional. The true shape should be a much calmer rolling programme of maintenance and replacement. If roads were in good repair and well maintained, reactive repairs could be all but eliminated.

Wider consequences

As we have already discussed with the planning applications and education there may be wider consequences to the service provided. This may mean that dealing with the services as transactional in isolation risks making the systems mistake of optimising the transactions to the detriment of the system as a whole.

Treating complex as transactional

All these services given as examples and many other complex services may well have transactional aspects to them. The service may involve applications, appointments, requests, visits, phone calls etc. Having a transactional component does not make a service transactional.

The argument must be made the other way too. A complex service may contain a transactional component while still being complex, but it is not the case that studying demand is of no value. Moving to a more sophisticated model does not necessarily make the simpler model redundant.

Treating complex systems as transactional and assuming that we have to study demand is a simplification error. We can think that we are making progress and find that we are actually making things worse.

Chapter 19

Inside In

I'm in with the "In" crowd.

I go where the "In" crowd goes.

Until recently the analysis of an organisation started from within and then spread into the world, this can be called "inside out". Seddon suggests that organisations are defined by the demand from the outside, so we should look at the work from the "outside in". Swapping from inside out to outside in is simply moving the camera position while still seeing the same scene. We need to go further to realise that the boundary between the organisation delivering the service and the service users is so blurred now that we should look at organisations as "inside in".

Lyrics from the song 'The In Crowd' by Billy Page.

Inside out

When we look inside out we decide what service we can provide, then we determine who can benefit from the service. Deciding how to deliver the service follows this and only then do we look at how much the user will benefit. I'm sure the reader will have often thought that certain companies and public sector organisations don't seem to be run for the benefit of the customers at all. It wasn't too long ago that high street banks would only open to 3.30pm, meaning that anyone with a job would have difficulty getting to the bank for an appointment.

We all know the systems that seem to foil the user from getting the service from the organisation because the processes are designed for the convenience of the people in the organisation with no thought for the user.

A patient was telling me that in order to get their hospital appointment they were sent a letter with a date and time to attend the clinic. The patient couldn't make that time so they called the number on the letter. The nurse answered and said that if they couldn't attend that appointment, another letter with an alternative appointment time would be generated and sent. The patient asked what would happen if they again couldn't make that second appointment. The nurse replied that a third letter would be sent. Again the patient asked what if they had to decline that appointment. The nurse said that if they couldn't make three suggested appointments, then they would be taken off the list and they would have to make another visit to their GP to request another clinic appointment. The patient was a little shocked at that and naturally asked if they could schedule an alternative appointment while on the phone. The nurse informed them that it wasn't possible since that wasn't the procedure.

Organisation defines value

In these inside out organisations the value is created internally and value is given out when requested. There are some circumstances when this is appropriate. As Henry Ford once said, "If I had asked my customers what they wanted, they would have said a faster horse."

The verdict on the value of the product or the service is left to the public after the service is delivered. If you didn't like it the first time around, don't buy another one.

Outside in

A more useful method is to reverse the view and look at the services from the point of view of the demands placed by customers. This is part of Seddon's method of looking at demand to see how well the organisation is able to meet it.

In this situation we study demand to determine the type and frequency. This analysis is then compared against the capability of the organisation to deliver against that demand. This method is most useful in transactional services.

Value deduced from demand

The value of the service is deduced from the demand. If there is a significant level of wasteful contacts then the service needs work. A low level of wasteful contacts does not necessarily mean there isn't room for improvement, but a high level always means there is a long way to go.

It is the value contacts that determine what people value and want. This is compared to the purpose of the organisation to ensure we are doing the right thing. In my experience working with clients this purpose step should not come first since it nearly always turns into a talking shop where the participants bring their assumptions and belief to the session, making the purpose closer to the waffle filled mission and values we saw in Chapter 2.

After demand, the flow of work is studied to determine where the waste, errors, delays and rework are. Combining this with a measurement of the capability of the organisation to deliver against the value contacts gives an idea of how the service can be redesigned to meet the value contacts, eliminate the waste contacts, errors, rework and delays and also to encourage the work to flow.

But given our complex services, this series of steps is not enough. We have seen that this is a good method for transactional services but with the blurred boundaries of these systems it is often hard to even identify the demand coming from outside. This makes it difficult to even start along this path.

Blurred boundaries

Central to both the inside out and the outside in views is the idea that we can clearly identify the inside and distinguish it from the outside.

Who is on the inside?

When we think of a local council and a community and the concepts of inside out and outside in, it begs the question, "Who is on the inside?" With both inside out and outside in, it is assumed that the council is the inside and the community is the outside. The public on the outside goes knocking on the door of the council and the staff on the inside provide services.

It could easily be argued the other way that the community is the inside and the council are the outside. The council staff come into the community to provide services. The community invites the council in by electing the councillors who in turn appoint the officers who run the services. But this also misses the mark.

The real situation is that councils and communities are part of each other. The council is elected by the community to run services on behalf of the people, but who are the council? They are members of the community they serve. And given that many council services are delivered by community groups, church groups and local charities, it is often the community who deliver their own services. And of course with the Big Society policy this is being encouraged more and more by the government.

So the distinction between the inside and the outside is a false one. So too therefore is the distinction of demand that comes from the outside.

The council is part of the community that delivers services for the community, to the community, by the community. Or at least, that is how it should be.

Inside in
Customers are on the inside of the community

So given that the service users are on the inside and the council is on the inside, then we need to move beyond inside out and outside in to the concept of "inside in" where value is defined by, for and with the community.

The council should not define value. Neither is value defined by outside demand. So how do we get a handle on value in an inside in service? The only way is that instead of following the work we must follow the customer.

Inside in all public services

This argument holds true not just for councils, but also for health care, transport, planning and just about every public service. We are in a democracy so our nation, regions and communities should be able to decide the services we provide to ourselves. We get the services we ask for.

	Value in work	Value in customer
Simple, linear, transactions	Inside Out (study products)	Not possible - when customer is at the centre it is never simple
Complex services	Outside In (study demand)	Inside In (follow customer)

Chapter 20

Follow the customer

*The customer is the locus of value
and value stays with them.*

Taking the inside in view of delivering services, it is not productive to rely on examining demand as our primary method of inferring value. This is simply because in complex human services, unlike transactional services, there is not the volume of discrete, classifiable demand. We have to look closer to the customer for some indication of value.

A team of health visitors caring for a population of elderly people in their homes is satisfying a need, but there is no way to classify that demand in the same way as if you could listen to calls into a contact centre. Each of those people will have different needs and likes that the visitors will have to take into account. Mrs Jones needs help with cooking but can get around the house quite well and doesn't like anyone who talks too much, while Mr Smith has incontinence but has a wicked sense of humour.

Understanding

It is the understanding of the patients that comes from daily contact that goes to give a good service. There are often budget constraints that force health visitors to try to see too many patients in a day. This prevents understanding and can lead to situations where some people are being put to bed at 5pm simply because otherwise the visitor can't get around to everyone in an evening. Also the case where a woman had 32 different carers in two weeks.[*]

This need for human contact and the growth of a relationship between the service user and the professional is at the core of complex human services.

Co-ordination

There is also the complication of co-ordination between agencies that characterises complex human services. Social work, chronic disease care, adult social care, education and many other services all require the interaction of many different agencies to deliver good services.

Family .

Very often the service user's family is heavily involved in giving care, making decisions about care or both. Having a good relationship with the family can be as important as the relationship with the recipient of the service. When decisions are being made, if the family does not understand or is against any changes to provision, it can cause stress to the service user and the family and will make it harder to provide effective service.

Communication

Communication is key. Staff and management must communicate in a timely, effective and appropriate manner with service users, families, other agencies and the public in general about the state of a service.

---

[*] http://www.guardian.co.uk/society/2011/jun/20/home-care-elederly-human-rights

Value is being near the customer
Value in the relationship

We can see that the value is in the relationship between the service giver and the service user. Whereas in a transactional service, the value was in the work and if the work was done away from the requester of the service, as long as the work was done quickly and correctly, the service user was happy. In complex human services, you can't do much, if anything, away from the service user. In fact it is an indicator that if work moves too far from a user in such situations then the value falls away until it is worthless.

As the distance increases so the personal relationship decreases, as does the understanding of the service user.

Examples of this are where social workers, doctors and police officers spend considerable portions of their day filling in forms away from the beneficiaries of their respective services.

When accompanying a friend to accident and emergency I noticed that the doctors and nurses spent a lot of time on computers in the centre of the department and not in the cubicles with patients. I asked one of them what they were up to and they said that they were trying to get patients beds in the hospital, filling in forms, requesting diagnostics, and all on terrible systems that took ages to respond.

Customer creates value

Further to the fact that value is created when near the customer, it is also often the customers that creates value themselves. In the example of a seven year-old that is not attending school, it will only be the child's parents who change their habits to get the pupil to school. This may happen with the support of an educational welfare officer, but in the end it is the parents who have to deliver the result.

If clients don't feel part of the solution then they are less likely to participate and there is probably going to be no improvement in their situation. Clients are an essential part of the change and so the solution and its continuing sustainability will rely upon them.

Section 5

Take Action

Chapter 21

Create your own models

Ideas shaped by others are
necessarily short of the mark
when applied to your system.

Models

A model is a simplification of reality that helps us understand the most important aspects of a system and thus guides us to action to improve the system in an effective way.

If the model is not a simplification it is redundant, if it does not bear similarity to reality it is misleading, if it does not give understanding it is obscure, if it does not guide action it is pointless and if that action does not generate improvement then the model is dangerous.

A good model is also one that can be adapted.

Models of complex human systems

In complex human systems models break down very quickly. They rapidly become as complex as the system they are trying to describe. This is because of the presence of the human aspect.

Models of physical systems, e.g. the climate or the solar system, are complex and may be chaotic in nature, but they don't contain as their parts, ever more complex systems. The solar system contains lumps of rock, liquid and gas, all of which are simpler than the system that contains them. In contrast a complex human system contains people, who taken individually, can be as difficult to understand as the systems they work in and use.

Deming understood this and this is why one of the four parts of his System of Profound Knowledge is psychology.[*]

The problem comes when the application of the model to the system and the people within it start to interact. This may be seen as resistance or avoidance. This leads to the whole study of intervention theory, which boils down to "How can I get them to accept my model?"

When a model for improvement encounters resistance, we typically think about either changing the method of engagement or changing the model. These reactions are both single-loop learning. There is resistance to the classroom training so we change the model that we train or we teach the same model in the workplace. In doing this we haven't challenged the assumption that we need to start with a model of the system.

In rejecting a need for a model, we obviate the need to teach people the model before we can start. The classic and most recent improvement techniques such as Six Sigma, Lean and Systems Thinking exhibit this trait; you can't start before you learn the model.

No instant pudding

Deming said that there is "no instant pudding". He meant that there is no trick you can bring from the outside that will always work in every system to produce improvement. The implication is that you have to work hard to understand and improve your own system and you shouldn't expect to be given a simple answer.

---

[*] The other three parts are Appreciation for a System, Knowledge of Variation and Theory of Knowledge.

In a *Horizon*[*] episode about Fermat's Last Theorem from 1998, the mathematician Andrew Wiles describes mathematics as being like entering a dark mansion. You enter the first dark room and you spend months fumbling round in the blackness bumping into the furniture until you get an idea of the layout. Finally, you find the light switch, turn on the light and you can see all the things you were tripping over all this time. Then you head off into the next dark room.

Organisations are worse than mathematical mansions because everyone thinks the light is on and they already know where the furniture is. In fact they are generally mistaken but their confidence leads them to stride into a room they think they know whereupon they smash their shins on things they never knew existed.

The mathematician has the caution of exploring unknown territory; while the public sector manager has the boldness of thinking they already know the lay of the land.

No formula

At this point in the book I make no apology that I can't give a formula for improvement or cutting costs. What this book contains is something more important. It gives a reason to and a way to better solve problems. And it is problem solving that is the key to improvement. Good problem solving is also sustainable since the next situation after the austerity regime will be different in detail and perhaps character, but the need for problem solving will never go away.

Principles

When formulating hypotheses it is useful to lean on some tried and tested principles. These principles are what underlie the tools that are evident in many of the improvement techniques popular today.

---

[*] *Horizon* is a BBC television series that explores new research in science and technology.

Use these principles to formulate your own hypotheses in your system. You will notice that these are the things we have been discussing so far in the book

- ◆ **Value to the customer**
- ◆ **Flow and pull**
- ◆ **Motivation is intrinsic**
- ◆ **Systems**
- ◆ **Variation**
- ◆ **Behavioural pressures**
- ◆ **Measures**

Application of principles

When we take a principle and apply it we have a local technique. If we document that local technique so others can repeat it then it becomes a tool. Using a tool without understanding the underlying principle is copying and dangerous.

Techniques

Many sources

There are many sources of tools and techniques. These include Lean, Six Sigma, TQM, Systems Thinking, Deming and the Toyota Production System. In the future there will be many more that come along. Some will endure and some will fade away.

Examples include 5S, Value Stream Mapping, Statistical Process Control and the 5 Whys.

How to use tools

When evaluating a new tool the need is to quickly identify:

1. **The principle that underlies the technique**
2. **Whether it is applicable to your system**

3. **How much you need to adapt the tool to make it effective**

4. **The resource needed to implement the experiment(s) that will give the answers to all of the above**

The HELP technique is essential to this process.

Every fad, model and method that comes along, in its own way illuminates a new or an age old principle that is valuable to apply. What the HELP technique does is give you a way of evaluating the principles from each new trend to see if they apply successfully to improve your system.

For example, the technique of pull signals – or kanban – can be applied almost anywhere, but how do we know whether it will be successful in our system? By formulating a testable Hypothesis, running a small Experiment, we can Learn and then take our new knowledge and Put it into Practice.

In a similar way we can test the principles and tools of the new theories and techniques as they arise and so we become free of the fads that come and go. Moreover, we can take from the passing trends only those new or rediscovered principles and techniques which will help us. This removes the state of hopping from one fad to the next which firstly, gives the staff the feeling that management don't know what they believe and secondly, means that the staff have no confidence in the current activities.

Learn how to learn

In order to make best use of the resources available to us we first need to know what the resources are.

Sources

Tools – *as described in books or case studies*

Case studies – *books, conferences, networking and visits*

Training – *internal, peer organisations and consultancies*

Reading – *books, journals and the internet*

Action – *most powerful method*

Create your own model
Combining tools, principles and learning

In combining principles, examples from other organisations and a method to learn by taking action you have a very powerful method for sustainable improvement. You will no longer be subject to the changeable weather of new fads and methods, instead you can see them for what they are; an opportunity to learn something new and a way to see old principles from a new vantage point. Seeing the likes of Six Sigma, Lean, Systems Thinking and their ilk in this way means you get the best out of them without having to swallow them whole. But it does mean you have to become a student of improvement and how it applies to your system. It also changes the way to evaluate tools and case studies. A typical response to a description of a tool or case study is this:

"They got great results with that tool/model/method. We should do that too."

The new response will be more like:

"They got great results with that tool/model/method. What are the principles that underlie that? Do we suffer from the same or similar problems that they did? Can it be adapted to suit us? Given the hypothesis that it will help, what experiment(s) will we need to run to reliably determine whether it really is for us? Then how can we take what we have learned and embed it into the work?"

It is deeper thinking and more work at the beginning but in the long term this way of formulating an evaluation will uncover both the unprofitable and the profitable avenues more quickly and effectively. Note especially that we test with experiments not leaving conclusions to supposition.

Chapter 22

Subtle interventions

Improvement seems to have become more complicated as the years have passed.

Ever more complex and unwieldy programmes are sold to unsuspecting organisations. Staff must attend copious training; they must win belts and learn myriad tools. Change teams must be appointed that sit outside the normal management structures. Sometimes there are matrix management systems where staff report to more than one manager and then also to the change facilitator in their area.

We must give up change for the sake of change; change as a programme or a set of tools; change as management reshuffle; and change as training. Change is only worthwhile if it is improvement. We must go back to improving the work to deliver value to the customer. We design the system of work to deliver value and the structures and measures follow from the design of work and its reason. Tools and training are pulled in where necessary, but the core driver is staff solving problems supported by management and resourced by upper management who also have a responsibility to see and communicate the system as a whole.

No resistance to change, just resistance to change programmes

Many millions of words have been written about the resistance to change. This is a distraction. There is no resistance to change. If someone were to acquire £10 million, that person's life would be changed forever. How many people would be resistant to accepting that money, no strings attached?

So people are not resistant to improvement, but they are resistant to the modern change programme. Change programmes often involve doing things that seem pointless to staff who can already see stupid things happening all around them that nobody is asking them about.

Staff want things to get better. Moreover, the service ethos in the public sector means that there is a great desire to better serve the public.

Don't want things to be done to them

Staff want to participate actively in improvement. They resent being told what to do by managers who have just arrived or consultants with their pet method under their arm that they are going to roll out by hook or by crook. Staff do the work every day and they are the experts in that. They feel they should have the biggest say when that work comes to change. They are not only in the right about that, but the staff have the most interesting things to say about what should and should not be changed.

Fear of the unknown change programme

When a new change programme comes to town, staff rightly fear that it will mean redundancies and cuts in service.

If the work is improved, massive savings to budgets can be made fairly easily and in better times that can be released as capacity to do other work. Unfortunately there is no way to promise that in the current climate there will be no job cuts to achieve the budget tightening required; though job losses can be reduced.

There is always a perception that most new change programmes have been done already, and since most are based on the same incorrect principles of focusing on individual staff members and management structures, this is normally true.

I was talking to a senior council officer and I was asking him about the budget cuts that his authority will have to find. He thought it would be between £15 million and £30 million. On a budget of £250 million, that is significant. The conversation turned to the large housing stock that the authority looks after. I asked what they were doing to save money. He told me that they had had a management reshuffle and that they were getting the maintenance staff on mobile working. So they were messing with management and adding technology costs. I asked if anyone was looking at how the work was being done. Was there the possibility of improvement in delivering the front line services like maintenance or rent collection? He looked at me as if I were from another planet.

Don't create a programme office or champions

While organisations do need outside support to find a new way of looking at systems and work, internal programme offices can be a distraction. In the same way that management has ceded staff development to Human Resources to the detriment of staff and their development, management have also given away responsibility to change offices and internal champions. Local managers and supervisors must take and be given the responsibility to improve their areas in concert with other areas. It is then the upper management who have the view of the system as a whole who should orchestrate the wider improvement. Other branches should not be needed. For who else but management is responsible for the system of work? If they are not responsible then they should not be there.

Change is emergent

When we start with the end in mind, the results of improvement are unpredictable. We open the system to innovation and to structures and ways of working that may not be foreseen. We can apply patterns and see shadows of other systems in ours, but true radical change emerges from the study of customer value, the system and the ability to deliver. Redesigning work from the top down, with the prejudices of learned thinking will not result in the best solution. We must go to where the work is done with an open mind to see what we will find and then act upon that.

Work is like science in that respect. The scientist that tries to mould the universe to her pet theory will be badly disappointed. Instead the great scientist observes, learns, then produces hypotheses about the world, which when tested will help her learn more. She then cycles round to produce more revealing suppositions, which in turn suggest more penetrating experiments.

We must act more like the scientist.[*]

Growing crystals

It is the job of management to create the concentration of enquiry about the work that will cause the crystals of innovation to start to grow. They need to supply a seed and they need to keep the concentration of the solution high to provide enough material to add to the crystal.

The seed is asking different questions and the concentration of the solution is providing ongoing support to improvement efforts by staff. To stretch the analogy, the staff are the material that form new, beautiful crystal formations, and while we can describe the micro structures of the new forms, the macro structures are unpredictable. They are emergent.

Support networking as and when it develops

As people start working on the work, they will want to share what they are doing. In addition, others in separate areas will hear of what is going on and wish to join in or do similar things in their areas.

This is where management must support efforts to network. The emphasis is on support rather than coercion. It is true that sometimes

---

[*]This is certainly not a call for "scientific management" as described by Frederick Winslow Taylor. I would call his method numerical management not scientific.

management want to spread improvement as far and as fast as possible. This urge should be resisted. Eventually people will contact each other and when they do, it will be far more effective than being forced together before they are ready.

With modern collaboration tools based on web technologies, networking can be facilitated easily and cheaply. However, nothing can replace getting together and talking. This should be encouraged.

Ask a different question

We suggested that the seed in the crystal was to ask different questions. It will be informative to note what questions we are asking at the moment that are producing the dysfunctional working and substandard performance.

The usual formula for planning work is, "How many people do we need to do the work that is coming in?" This is a simple mathematical question and in the end it does need to be answered, but the problem is that managers ask these questions first and never go any deeper. Questions about the quantity of work coming in don't ask about the type of work, i.e. is it a wanted contact or a wasteful contact? Similarly the question about how long it takes to do work doesn't ask if all the steps in the process produce value for the customer. It is also inevitably a question about how long it takes to do a small part of the process, e.g. how long does it take to deal with a telephone call? Customers don't care about the length of the call; they care about the total end-to-end time to get their repairs done. If they have to call ten times to chase and complain it won't make them feel better if each call is efficiently handled (efficient according to the call centre); they would prefer one effective call that led to a quick or convenient repair.

The new, subtle, less direct form of intervention is based around asking better questions. These questions are asked of staff and the answers are given a high priority. It should be clear that the investigations to uncover the answers are important to the organisation and not a passing thought.

Is our service transactional or complex?

Our first big hypothesis is to ask if our service is transactional or complex. In the case that we believe it to be transactional this forces us to look at the work coming in. We must ask which are wasteful contacts and which are wanted contacts. Typically the level of wasteful contacts is much higher than people expect.

In the case that we believe our service to be complex then we should move to the next question.

What do our customers value?

Customer value derives from seeing the service from the customers' point of view. Customer value is essential to judge the answer to the next question.

What are we here to do?

This strikes at the heart of the meaning of the organisation. It is a question of having a reason. In a transactional service wanted contacts will point to the reason for the service. In a complex service we have less to go on and so have to turn to fast-fail problem solving to guide us. Starting by formulating a reason is to start by guessing.

How are we doing?

This is a question of ability to deliver. The more complex way to phrase the question is, "How well are we meeting the need of customers by delivering customer value and achieving our reason?" Aspects of variation due to a system should be part of the answer to this one. We can see that all these questions build upon each other.

What caused us to be like this in the first place?

Before we can get to the redesign phase we must look at the behavioural pressures that caused the dysfunction. This will be targets, bonuses, inspection, process and many other things. Unless we remove these pressures, we will inevitably revert to the old ways.

How can we redesign to maximise value and remove waste?

This is the question that pulls all the previous questions together. It should not be asked before answering all the questions above. The design should focus on delivering value; this will in turn eliminate the waste.

People must unlearn before they can learn

There is a barrier to some of these ideas. That barrier is that people don't like to be told that they have been doing things wrong for so long. When they hear about similar changes in other organisations they laugh and can't believe how silly people in those other places have been. How can those others not see the waste and how much they are annoying their customers? But tell people that they are doing the same things and they will dig in and tell you that you are wrong. Chris Argyris writes that people must unlearn before they can learn.

Can't be told about themselves

When presenting to one set of people I will tell stories about different organisations since people seem to get that. Call centre managers get stories about bankers and vice versa. Tell call centre managers that their measures, incentives and processes are wrong, even with solid case studies, and they will baulk at the idea that they are suffering from the same illusions. They will disbelieve you and set their minds against what you are saying.

See for themselves

The only way to get people to learn is to first use other sectors as examples then have them see for themselves. They must be asked the questions as described above and then given tasks that mean they go to the place where the work is done to find the answers. They won't find the answers in a conference room. They must get out on the ambulances, ride the dustcarts, go to the wards, sit with the benefits officers and accompany the social workers on visits. What they will typically find is that a lot of time is not spent where it should be. The social workers spend time in front of computers rather than with clients, but the team investigating need to see this rather than hear about it.

Now open to new ways

Only once the team have been to where the work is done and seen the real situation will they start to get what needs to be undone. Only then will they be open to new thinking. This process cannot be shortened. Of course there will be a few who already know it, and a further group that will get it quicker than others; the point is you need the majority to see what is wrong before you can make progress as a team to dump the old thinking and be open to move on.

Don't start a big programme

The temptation when upper management alight on a new method is that there must be a big programme announced with all the training, fanfare and communications that those efforts entail.

Ask the right questions of the right people and so much more can be achieved in a much shorter time scale.

Programmes suck up resources, people and time. Investigating a few pertinent questions can be surprisingly quick. Programmes can last years, give nothing and be abandoned. Doing the investigations described can get results in weeks. You can start your first productive HELP cycles within a fortnight.

Anything you start can be stopped

Programmes start, so programmes stop. New programmes are started. The cycle of management fads moves on. This is one of the things that staff hate.

We are not here to initiate a programme. The intention is to change thinking. That is something that can't be started and stopped. You can create the right environment for it to happen at the beginning, but you can't change people's minds, only show them some new ideas. They will change their own minds.

Once people have a new way of thinking then they won't go back. You can stop a programme but you can't stop people if they think in a new way.

This shift is hard to start directly and once going impossible to stop.

Culture is not in programmes or projects

Culture is emergent from the environment created by management. If the environment concentrates on the work, how the work delivers value to customers and aligns with the reason, people will get behind that naturally since that is what they have wanted to do since they arrived. The culture of achievement follows naturally.

Save money on t-shirts

Some programmes spend amazing amounts of money on logos, newsletters, t-shirts, pens and mugs. Does this enhance value to the customer? No. So why do they do it?

Sustain by revisiting

The way to sustain this change is to get out of the way of the staff and start to support them. Once they make changes, they will see benefit for the public and that will spur them on to continue. Managers will have to become expert in supporting the staff's efforts and occasionally re-asking the original questions to refocus attention on what is important.

HELP becomes a habit

The HELP cycle should be supported as part of the daily work. As the technique becomes embedded the daily meetings can be reduced, but only once staff start spontaneously using HELP on their own to solve problems.

Learning goes into the work

The way that organisations learn is by putting the lessons into the work. The last two steps of HELP are Learn and Put into Practice. We learn from our experiments then put those lessons into the everyday tasks, processes and procedures. The work is the organisation's memory.

Writing documents and putting them in drawers or hiding them on servers is not learning; it is simply a waste of time. Nobody ever reads those documents or opens those files. Those who do are typically new starters who are told to read them to understand how things work. They find that the documentation hasn't been updated for months or years and that there is barely anything useful or relevant in there. They eventually get to the work where they have to relearn everything from the people who do the work.

This is why, when we want to learn about how the work is done, going to the place that the work is done is the only reliable way.

Projects and kaizen blitz won't help

Management love boxed methods. They crave a simple, bounded solution. Come and do this set of things and all will be well.

Kaizen blitz or kaizen events are typically five days where you get a cross-disciplinary team in a room and they very quickly go through a value stream to identify waste, redesign the process and put in place quick fixes. The problem being that the changes are local, the time allowed doesn't give room for proper understanding of deeper problems and the change is by definition jerky and lumpy. Staff wait for the next kaizen event to come around so they can lurch forward again.

We are trying to change long-term thinking, initiate improvement as a part of the daily work so it happens all the time and also give an appreciation of the system as a whole.

Improvement is addictive

Once improvement starts and staff and customers can see the results, the process can become addictive. The release from former regimes of repression of ideas can lead to a gush of new ways of looking at the way the system operates. The only thing management need to do is to resist the temptation to slow it down. Management still have the responsibility for seeing the system as a whole, but that should not be an excuse for rejecting ideas. Instead, managers should communicate the wider view to staff to assist them with generating better ideas. The HELP cycle will give the practical way to test ideas that will either improve the system or not. It is that practical mechanism that will teach staff what works and what doesn't. That interaction with the work and the tangible success it brings is self-sustaining as long as management are there to give it resource and they are not there to criticise and block.

Start small, grow exponentially

It is very hard to persuade people to start a new method across an organisation. Even if that were desirable, it would violate the principle of HELP. The first instance of looking at our reason and customer value is a pilot or the first experiment.

The way to grow the instances is to start small and grow exponentially.

First instance

There will be a natural area to start. This will be where there are open minds or a particularly enthusiastic manager who is already asking to do something similar, has done something of his or her own volition or is obviously keen to try something new.

Often people start where the service might seem to suit, so more transactional areas seem attractive. For example, the pharmacy or a diagnostic service in the NHS or benefits or refuse collection in local authorities. But if the enthusiasm is greater in a more complex service then that is the place to start. In fact, an early success in a complex service such as cardiac surgery or social services can head off the criticism that sometimes comes from starting somewhere more transactional where people will assume it must have been easy.

Let enthusiasm pull application rather than pushing implementations because of perceived practicality.

HELP is fractal

A fractal is something that is self-similar at different scales. The classic example is described in a paper[*] by the inventor of fractals, Benoît Mandelbrot entitled *How Long Is the Coast of Britain? Statistical Self-Similarity and Fractional Dimension*. In it he determined that if you are looking down at the coast of Britain that it had a certain amount of jaggedness. The interesting thing was that the amount of jaggedness was the same if you were looking from a satellite, from a helicopter, standing on a beach or looking though a microscope. You would get different answers from the question, "How long is the coast of Britain?" because the smaller the scale the more jags you have to take into account. But the jaggedness didn't vary. In other words the coast of Britain was statistically self-similar at all scales.

A similar effect can be seen if you show a person a chart of stock prices. If you leave off the timescale, they will not be able to tell you whether the chart shows prices from yesterday, the last month or the last hundred years. The random looking fluctuations of the world's stock markets have a similar feel at all timescales.

HELP cycles have the same property. The steps of Hypothesis, Experiment, Learn, Put into Practice are the same whether you are working on your own personal work, across a team, a division, an organisation or a nation. It is self-similar at all scales.

---

[*]Benoît Mandelbrot, *How Long Is the Coast of Britain? Statistical Self-Similarity and Fractional Dimension. Science,* New Series, Vol. 156. Mp/ 3775/ (May 5, 1967).

This property is very helpful when applying HELP since it means that the fundamental structure still holds true at all levels of the organisation and beyond. This means that staff from different levels of the organisation can participate in HELP cycles and still contribute strongly because they don't have to learn a new problem solving technique.

HELP is scalable to any problem.

It also means that HELP cycles can overlap at many different scales at the same time, all contributing to each other and reinforcing one another. It is the case that people who cut their teeth on smaller HELP cycles start to see the bigger things that are wrong within the organisation and the cycles naturally tend to become larger over time. In these cases it is important to still encourage HELP to be applied at all scales as you proceed.

Create eagerness

In the same vein as choosing where to start, rather than have management decide where to move next, let the next area pull the new methods into it.

The way to let staff know is by creating eagerness in the rest of the organisation. Curiosity is too slow. You need to get creative here. It is tempting to have town hall meetings where we do dry PowerPoint presentations of projects that are supposed to inspire others to try it too.

Eagerness is aroused when people talk but don't give too much away. Try to encourage staff that are happy with the new situation to talk to others by mentioning results but not going into detail about what happened. The natural reaction of others is to ask how it was done. If they don't ask, you know they aren't interested. If they do, then that is your chance to hook them.

If you are a manager in an area that hasn't been part of the new method and you would like to try it, how about chatting to your staff about what went on in the other area? Tell them of the results the other area got. Then instead of announcing that your area will try it next, why not ask them if they would like similar results. It is useful to get staff to imagine a similar situation. For example, if you are the manager of a benefit service then you might tell your staff how the planning office managed to reduce their end-to-end time by 50% when they were targeted to reduce it by 5%. You might then discuss with your staff how it would be to reduce your average enquiry-to-payment time from 35 days to 16 days. Then shut up and let the staff ask how that would be possible. Given that they do so, you can easily move to the questions from above starting with, "What is important to our customers?" and moving on through the process.

Happy staff will naturally talk to their friends around the organisation and they should be encouraged to do so. As the word spreads, that eagerness needs to be followed up with action as upper management identify enquiries to do something similar.

Some tips can be taken from the world of marketing where viral techniques are becoming more and more popular to naturally spread the word across the world. We are not necessarily talking about making funny videos, but a natural encouragement of word of mouth and networking will pay dividends. A recommendation from a peer is far more powerful than a command from the top of the hierarchy.

Use email to send round some of the new results from the first few pilots and leave a teaser as to how they were achieved with a way to respond if people want to know more. Hopefully these emails will be forwarded around until a buzz is created.

It is more effective to use less formal methods to spread the word since this avoids the resistance to change programmes that comes from the more orthodox methods of communication. People pull the new ways of doing things towards them rather than being pushed into them.

Results come more quickly than might be thought in this way. It is true that initially it might seem slow, but as the word spreads, it will feed on itself. The rate of take-up will accelerate. This process can be helped along.

Invite others to participate

On your first pilot, invite from two to four outsiders from other areas to participate. You will not only add fresh views with ideas from outside but will also be assisting the spread of the new ways of thinking.

Do this for every instance and two to four outsiders in every new implementation will cause that exponential process to explode. Moreover, you will not just be relying on hearsay to pass on the news; they will be independent people who have actually participated in an area that has had success, so the report will carry more weight.

Make it clear that participants from outside will be expected to take the questions and ways of thinking back to their areas and that they will also be expected to make an immediate start. Momentum is an important property to capitalise on. Just as inertia can stall a movement, in the same way building on momentum can accelerate the spread of new ideas.

Don't roll out, let eagerness pull

The temptation will be to roll out the programme. The better strategy is to create eager people who pull interventions. As they being to show enthusiasm, ensure that they get to be the outside participants in the next area's starting experiment. Let people attend others' daily HELP sessions and statement of reason sessions.

Eagerness will draw people in, so they will pull themselves into the new way rather than having management formally roll out a programme.

Management commitment must be solid

Just because we don't have a formally announced programme does not mean that management do not have a key role to play in sustaining interest in interventions and good support of investigations. HELP implementations will drift, and swift and skilled management intervention is needed to keep efforts on track.

We only need to look at Toyota, who for decades were the exemplar of these kind of techniques, to see that loss of management focus can quickly lead to a previously world-beating organisation damaging its hard won reputation.

Answers to questions are a clear priority

As said previously, the investigations to answer the new questions must have a clear priority. There must be no ambiguity that the system as a whole and customer value are the keys to how the organisation will operate and deliver in the future.

Subtle doesn't mean weak

Being subtle in the way we do interventions does not mean being weak. The intervention is more oblique but the direction is solid, and that must be communicated to staff so they are under no illusion that while this is not a formal programme, there is no less commitment to the outcomes for customers. This is underpinned by the knowledge that giving customers the value they seek will benefit budgets, staff, morale and the organisation as a whole.

It is also important that there is no duplicity in this method. Staff should never be lied to. Nor should they ever have information deliberately withheld from them. While the methods to create eagerness might use a little mystery to try and draw in new people, in no way should this be treated as an opportunity to hide things from staff. If they ask, be open and honest. It is better to be forthcoming with information than forcing staff to enquire after it.

Give responsibility and credit to staff

As you proceed, ensure that you are giving responsibility to staff to firstly act as they see fit within the confines of the principles of customer value and secondly to learn for themselves using the HELP cycle and other methods.

Credit is important for staff to celebrate successes. Often flabbergasted members of the public will start writing notes and sending flowers because they will not be able to believe the service they are getting. Ensure that these expressions of gratitude are shared with the team. Management thanks is good, but nothing says well done better than a positive response from the public. Ensure everyone knows that this is a collective result. One social worker getting flowers is likely to be the result of many dozens of staff pulling together to improve that service. Don't diminish their personal joy, but you can bring everyone together to share that thanks without dampening the individual's pleasure at being thanked.

Chapter 23

Start today

Let's get going.

The steps to improving your system have been dotted around the book so far. It is time to lay them out explicitly.

1. **Review the principles**

2. **Identify value to the customer**

3. **Follow the customer**

4. **State the reason for your service**

5. **Apply HELP cycles**

While you are doing all this you need to communicate both failures and successes. The successes will create the eagerness in others to have a go and the honest disclosure of failures will reduce their fear to try.

1.   Review the principles

Let's relist the principles from Chapter 21:

♦   **Value to the customer**

♦   **Flow and pull**

♦   **Motivation is intrinsic**

♦   **Systems**

♦   **Variation**

♦   **Behavioural pressures**

♦   **Measures**

Your first hypothesis will probably be based upon one of the principles listed above.

2.   Identify the value to customers

Taking the customers' point of view defines customer value. If people complain of slow service then one of their values will be end-to-end time. Any time payment of money is involved, end-to-end time is a customer value. If there is some decision to be made, for example planning or benefit entitlement, then getting that decision right first time is essential. If members of the public have to come for an appointment or someone has to visit their homes, then convenience is normally an important factor.

Don't spend time or money on expensive surveys. Normally customer value is self-evident and should become more so as we take it into the next step.

It is useful to divide value into:

♦   **Essential – the plane must not fall from the sky**

♦   **Expected – a seat on the aircraft**

♦   **Nice to have – local airport and a free in-flight drink**

♦   **Luxury – seats that turn into beds or a gym on board the plane**

With these classifications you can judge whether what you are planning is important enough to work on first. You should always prioritise essential over expected and so on. Essential is normally about safety and expected is about the basic working of the service. It is not uncommon to see public services working on nice to haves like online access when it is still taking weeks to get service via the normal channels.

Recognise that this is a first pass and the customer value you determine will necessarily change as we follow the customer in the next step. Think of this step as a hypothesis of customer value which will be tested in the Examine Data phase of Follow the Customer.

3.   Follow the customer

It is worth repeating here that unlike in transactional services where the value is in the work, in complex services the value is near the customer so we follow the customer not the work.

Listen to the customer

To study the flow of value is to follow the customer.

Gather a team of mixed staff brought from all the areas through which the value flows. Then "be a customer". Simply pretend that you are a customer coming in and follow yourself along.

Keep it simple

This process mapping should be kept simple. Take a piece of paper divided into four columns and add the headings:

♦   **Process**

♦   **Problems**

♦   **Impact**

♦   **Pressures**

In the first column add the process step description; that might be an instruction or a decision. In the second, record any problems with this step such as the number that arrive that are not able to be dealt with – put real numbers here if possible. In the third column, put in any impact of the problems. If there is a cost put it in. Other impacts might be delay or rework. The fourth column is to record any behavioural pressures for the next step.

On the first pass along the process, concentrate on the main flow of value. You will find that most of the decisions are about dealing with errors or unclean information. These decision points are impeding the flow and we will design them out. It is not necessary at this stage to detail all the branches and sub-branches of the problems and resolution trees. It will suffice to get an idea of the complexity.

It is essential that you map the process end-to-end through whatever sections or departments might touch it.

Watch out for flow or the lack of it. Look for handovers, delays, waits, errors, inspection, checking, sign-offs, excessive decision trees, transportation and anything stopping work flowing. See them from the customers' point of view.

A value step is one that adds value for the customer. Everything else is waste.

While doing this, make sure that you are out where the work is done or where the customers are and not in a meeting room. Also don't waste time with mapping processes in any fancy software packages. They are quite hard to use and won't tell you anything more than pen, paper and sticky notes can.

Most importantly never forget the customer. It is easy to concentrate on the work in this step and completely forget about the customer.

4.   State the reason for your service

The reason is based on what is important to the customer.

Note that we don't start with the reason for the service. To do so would be presumptuous. The whole method is a big HELP cycle. As with all implementations of HELP we cycle round and never stop. Don't just apply the method once.

Don't take too long

The process of coming up with a reason for the service should be as short and as sweet as the eventual statement itself. Allow an hour, invite the initial group who studied the work and have a good facilitator to ensure that the group does not go off on tangents.

You may find useful the technique of asking people to write their version of the "reason we are here" on sticky notes in silence, then having them stick them up on the wall for everyone to read. Small sticky notes ensure that the statements are limited by space and everyone feels they get their version seen by all the others. The process can be kicked off much quicker like this. Announce the time limit at the start and reiterate the principle that good is what is useful now and that perfection will come in time. Hopefully, this will curtail flights of fancy, overly ambitious statements and excessive philosophising.

Don't involve too many people

A maximum in the group of 10–12 is preferable. Ensure that you have representatives from a fairly wide base of the areas that deliver this value so that all groups feel they have had representation.

Profile a customer

It can help to profile a typical customer. Sometimes you can use two or three to represent prominent or large sub-groups of your customer base.

The idea is to fix in the mind of the study group a particular person who uses the service. The person is constructed such that if the service is valuable to him or her, then the service is valuable to most of the other service users.

Think about:

♦   **Age**

♦   **Sex**

♦   **Wealth**

♦   **Education**

- ◆ **Location**
- ◆ **Family circumstances**
- ◆ **Likes**
- ◆ **Needs**
- ◆ **Disabilities**
- ◆ **Ethnic origin**

And anything else that is relevant to the service in question.

For example a 17-year-old male A-level student will be a good guide for a programme about youth sports participation, but a bad one for adult social care provision.

It can really help to pin up a photograph[*] and give the person a full name. The more real the character seems to the group, the more they will identify with the person and the more the character will inform the search for the reason for the service.

Revisit the customer and reason

The reason for the service is not fixed. The thinking that went into it is just as important as the words that you end up with. The way you think about your service or organisation will change as you learn about it and change it, so it may be appropriate to also change the reason for the service.

The statement is a guide, something to think back on to keep you on the right track. You might turn to it and find it no longer reflects the organisation or what you are here to do. You might find yourself taking decisions that are at odds with or grate against the stated reason. Don't assume that the decisions are wrong, they may well be, but ensure that the current statement of the reason is something that is still useful.

The statement of the reason is like a step in one of your processes. If it is no longer useful or relevant, change it or eliminate it.

---

[*] You can get copyright free photos on the internet.

Not right first time

Don't worry if you don't get the right statement of the reason immediately. It can take several iterations before a useful reason settles down. Remember the point is that it is useful as something to judge results, processes and measurements by. As long as it is useful, that is enough. Good enough to use now is sufficient. Perfection will come in time.

5. Apply HELP cycles

Action is learning. We cannot help seeing something new when we do something different.

In fact we have already been starting on a guided HELP cycle in going through the first four steps. They were building and testing hypotheses about your service before getting to the real action here. It might be worthwhile to relist the steps with the phase of HELP that they represent:

1. **Review the principles** - *Hypothesis about systems and people*

2. **Identify value to the customer** - *Hypothesis about the customer*

3. **Follow the customer** - *Examine date about the system and the customer*

4. **State the reason for your service** - *Hypothesis about the service as a whole*

5. **Apply HELP cycles** - *Start all over again*

We could have simply started by asking you to begin with any Hypothesis that you thought germane, but practice shows that a little guidance at the start will give results much more quickly. We are now ready to dive into the HELP cycles with no constraints and we can refer back to the first four steps for guidance at any time.

Use HELP

The hypotheses should be practical and testable. A Hypothesis that cannot be moved onto the Experiment / Examine data phase should be revisited or junked. If you can't test, it you can't learn from it. That is not to say that you may be able to test that hypothesis later on, but to waste time when there are always other ideas to test is folly.

You need time, money and skill to set up a proper experiment. Some experiments will be more intensive than others. Beware the huge, resource sucking experiment that promises everything, chances are that you can break it down or change it to make it more manageable. Recall the mantra of "fail fast, fail small".

Ensure that you are not changing too many things at once. Remember the NHS Bedfordshire study where they wanted to reduce the number of missed appointments? They had a number of techniques: receptionists would ask if patients could call if they couldn't come; nurses would ask patients to fill in their own appointment cards; they made the signs in the waiting rooms more positive. If they had done all of those things at the same time it would have been difficult to establish which had produced what effect. Recall also that they did try asking patients to write down a 4-digit appointment code which resulted in more missed appointments not fewer. What if they had run the 4-digit code trial at the same time as the other trials? They would have never have known that it was detrimental to results. Its negative effect would have been buried in the positive results of the other techniques.

You must put into practice what you learn from each cycle. The new practice must quickly become the new benchmark for the next experiment. Don't sit on good results, implement them immediately. This takes management commitment to follow through with HELP cycles. Not doing this will quickly lead to staff losing heart and wondering why they are bothering.

In a similar manner, once a HELP cycle is complete, move quickly onto the next. It is the repeated reapplication that creates the momentum and eventually will expand the scope and effect of the HELP cycles until they are covering the whole organisation.

If the hypothesis was disproved, it can often still be the basis of the next hypothesis. Recall the principle of diversity. Sometimes the opposite to conventional thinking is the thing that works. Be open minded and let people try things out without judgement. The results of a well-planned experiment will be much more instructive and useful than rejection from management.

Frequent and systematic

Learning needs to be frequent. In time it will become part of the work, woven into the fabric of the day so that it is indistinguishable from other tasks. But at first, action for learning needs to be structured into work by setting aside time for it.

A good start is a daily stand up meeting within the team where staff can start to share with everyone the observations they have made about things that might be improved. These should be noted and displayed prominently. Managers should be quiet during these initial sessions. They should not be tempted to explain away situations, procedures or policies at all. In these first few sessions any hint that managers are disapproving will very quickly shut down the flow of observations and ideas from staff, and clawing back trust will be almost impossible.

The stand up meetings should be about 10 minutes long. Mid-morning works well since it means people can get to work, sort out anything that is pressing first thing and then have the stand up meeting while they are still relatively fresh.

The meetings are held standing up since that helps promote brevity. When a group is standing they don't want to drag the meeting out like they would when all sat around a table. Also, just have the meetings in a space on the floor. No need to go into a room, unless not doing this would significantly disturb others in an open plan office. Not moving too far also minimises the disruption to the participants' work. In addition, a group standing up for 10 minutes every morning will generate talk amongst other teams in a big office, which is a great way to get some eagerness going.

It is worth repeating that the bulk of the input should come from staff and not from managers and the ideas are not to be analysed at this stage, simply recorded. Flip chart paper is fine for recording the ideas and these can be stuck up somewhere close by.

Hold these meetings every day for a week, and on the Friday, review what has been recorded for that first week. In that fifth meeting, decide as a group what three things they are going to try and fix in the next week. The homework over the weekend is to come up with ways to fix the problems.

In the Monday meeting ask for the solutions. Try and bring everyone into the discussion as far as possible.

Emphasise that you need to take action to change something. Theorising in this meeting is fine to a limited extent, but the end goal is to come up with a trial action that can be implemented by the team in that week, which can be evaluated the following Monday.

The outputs you need are:

1. **What are we going to do?**
2. **Who is going to do it?**
3. **When are these actions going to take place?**
4. **How are we going to monitor the experiment?**
5. **How will we know if it worked?**
6. **If it works, what action will we take?**
7. **If it doesn't work, what action will we take?**

It is important that all these questions are answered since it is very easy to slip into assuming that solutions are final and that we jump to implementing non-reversible changes.

Theorising without action is worthless

The fact that we are about to take action is crucial. If the problem you are looking at means you have to go and ask permission or perform more analysis then pick another one. Eventually you will graduate to those types of problem, but for these first actions you must pick experiments that you can enact easily within the week. This will get the team going and into the feeling of doing something. Not taking action will embed the feeling that this is a talking shop where yet again, nothing gets done. Staff will feel that they are standing around for 10 minutes a day for nothing and they will feel cheated (again) and enthusiasm will wane.

Managers must avoid the temptation to modify the team's suggested experiment. They are there to support and to help the team learn, while remembering that means the team might be wrong sometimes. Let them be wrong; they will learn more from it.

The team will run the experiment for a week and then evaluate it. If it has worked, the change must be implemented immediately. Managers must ensure that this happens – this is where the support and providing resource comes in. Management jobs are starting to change from providing solutions and then ensuring that they are implemented as described, to facilitating the staff to come up with solutions and then supporting the testing and embedding of the answers.

During the first experiment the 10-minute meeting is held where further problems can be aired, but also part of the meeting can be given over to the experiment. This is not to see if the experiment is working, proper judgement can only happen at the end, but rather to see if any further assistance is required. Do they need more information, resource or removal of barriers?

Be flexible

The stand up meeting and timings described are suggestions. Each team may adapt them to their own circumstances. But be warned about changing things too much. Teams should start with the procedure described and then change details in line with the method. Try something, evaluate it and then implement what you learn in the same way as for improving the work.

You can apply HELP to how you run HELP. That is how and why HELP was changed from PDSA.

Sustained action is best

As this meeting format proceeds and develops you can accelerate the number of experiments that are run at the same time. As people see that management are serious about running with their ideas there will be a clamour to try lots of new things. This is good, but there must be a clear message that ideas are not sufficient on their own. There must also be a way to test them, with a way to evaluate that test and a plan to implement what is learned.

That is the scientific method.

Management of problem solving
Frequency

Use HELP in little chunks, often. It should get to the stage where staff are seeing problems and improvement opportunities every day, and you need to be able to implement them just as fast as they arise.

In the early stages, the staff will need a little prodding, so it is useful to make time in the 10-minute daily meeting to get 30-second updates on new Hypotheses, the progress of Experiments, what was Learned and actions to Put into Practice.

Encouragement

The frequent application of HELP will come to replace the performance appraisal. A consistent application will result in staff becoming more engaged in the work and managers understanding the work and how the staff perform it and relate to it much better. Managers need to be positive, especially about the Hypotheses that don't turn out to be correct. Those failures need to be turned into lessons for the proposer and the group to learn from. The most important lesson every time is that failures are constructive and we want more ideas so we can get to the gold.

Risk

Many people are worried that all this experimenting will get in the way of doing the work. This is a possibility, but it can be mitigated by skilful experimental design. Experiments that involve a lot of action away from the work should be redesigned to try to integrate the actions required back into the everyday work. For remember it is the work that is being studied and changed. This is a skill that is gained by a team as they proceed and it is helpful to get some outside support with this aspect.

The risk of improvement activity taking time from doing the day-to-day work also reduces as the first improvements start to be harvested since these improvements will release time from the work, thus leaving even more time for improvement. It rests on the management to trust that sticking the first foot in the door will lead to ever-increasing dividends.

How formal should HELP be?

Doing HELP should be as formal or informal as is required. Err on the side of less formal, lest managers and teams fall into the documentation trap. If a formal description is necessary then a single side of A4 should be sufficient. There is a technique known as "A3" where a side of A3 is used to describe a HELP cycle, but it is a bit heavy handed.

The stand up meetings should be the arbiter of how much recording is required. Again keep it informal at first and only add formality as is needed.

Documentation is only required when you want to communicate to others what you are doing or have done. The last thing that should happen is that people are judged by their HELP plans on a formal basis. Never should ideas for improvement be counted or scored. This will stop any progress dead in its tracks.

Aims of the HELP cycles

1. Improve the ability to give customers value

Take the customer value and turn it into measures. So "I want my benefits quickly" turns into a measure of end-to-end time. Take these measures and plot them on a control chart (SPC chart). You will probably find that while your demand is predictable, at first your ability to meet customer value is highly unpredictable.

If you have dozens of customer value measures you have probably confused customer value with some internal measures. Ensure that you are strict about what measures matter to the customer and that every measure spans the system as a whole. Don't measure parts of the process. The customer is only interested in service they get in its entirety.

2. Remove the behavioural pressures

As you walked the flow of work you will have identified behavioural pressures. Now is the time to start talking to upper management about them. You will need to be persuasive about how the behavioural pressures are distorting behaviour and worsening performance. Of course, if you have some upper and middle management on your team then this will be much easier.

3. Promote flow and pull

Armed with customer value, a reason, ability to deliver, a process map and a bevy of behavioural pressures to remove, you can now proceed to redesign your work. Aim to minimise handovers, to promote flow or implement pull.

Try to put as much expertise as near to the customer as possible. If the person who picks up the phone to a wanted contact can do the whole job before moving to the next wanted contact, that is perfect one-piece flow.

4. To give staff a voice and influence

HELP cycles will bring staff together with colleagues and managers to solve problems. Well managed, this process will gradually bring staff back to the point where they were when they first arrived in the organisation: keen to get things done. The systematic application of HELP gives structure to the ideas of staff and assists them to express themselves to peers and managers. Structured problem solving can be a very levelling exercise. Everyone is at the level of the problem and the hierarchy often melts away as the ideas start to flow. Good ideas can come from any level and it takes staff action, support from managers and commitment from senior management to enact the experiments needed to prove the ideas worthy. It is truly a team effort.

Afterword

I have no doubt that if all public sector bodies were to take the lessons and apply the principles in this book, we could together save public services and avoid the potential devastation that the government cuts promise. All it takes is action and dedication.

Where my clients have implemented the steps with persistence and enthusiasm they have had some amazing results. That is not to say that they (and I) have not had set backs and gone down blind alleys. But those missteps are how we learn and improve. It is through inaction that we stay where we are. It is only through action that we end up somewhere better than we could ever have expected.

So if you are still holding this book, please give it to a colleague to read and go and do something constructive before the public have no services left at all.

Good luck!

Rob Worth

Find out more

Web site

http://www.BeatTheCuts.com

You can find out more about how to "Beat the Cuts" at our website where there are blog posts, articles, podcasts and a forum to share your experiences.

Twitter

You can follow Rob Worth on Twitter at http://www.twitter.com/Rob_ Worth or using the twitter account @Rob_Worth

Worth Solutions Limited

More general information about Rob Worth and Worth Solutions Limited can be found at http://www.WorthSolutions.com

Bibliography

Systems thinking

Ackoff, Russell. *Management F-Laws: How Organizations Really Work*, Triarchy Press (2007).

Deming, W. Edwards. *Out of the Crisis*, MIT Press; 2nd edition (2000).

Deming, W. Edwards. *The New Economics For Industry, Government, Education*, MIT Press; 2nd Revised edition (2000).

Joiner, Brian. *The New Business Consciousness: Fourth Generation Management*, McGraw-Hill Professional, (1994)

Neave, Henry. *The Deming Dimension*, SPC Press, Inc. (1990).

Ohno, Taiichi. *Toyota Production System: Beyond Large-Scale Production*, Productivity Press, (1988).

Scholtes, Peter. *The Leader's Handbook: Making Things Happen, Getting Things Done*, McGraw-Hill Professional, (1998).

Seddon, John. *Freedom from Command and Control*, Triarchy Press (2005).

Seddon, John. *Systems Thinking in the Public Sector*, Triarchy Press (2008).

Shewhart, Walter Andrew. *Statistical Method from the Viewpoint of Quality Control*, New York: Dover (1939).

Statistical Process Control

Wheeler, Donald J. *Understanding Variation: The Key to Managing Chaos*, SPC Press, Inc.; 2nd edition (2000).

Motivation

Kohn, Alfie. *No Contest: The Case Against Competition*, Houghton Mifflin (1993).

Kohn, Alfie. *Punished by Rewards*, Houghton Mifflin (2000).

Pink, Daniel. *Drive: The Surprising Truth About What Motivates Us*, Canongate Books Ltd (2010).

General

Ambrose, Stephen E. *Band of Brothers*, Pocket Books (2001).

Argyris, Chris. *Knowledge for Action*, Jossey Bass (2003).

Covey, Stephen. *The 7 Habits of Highly Effective People*, Simon & Schuster Ltd (2004).

Harford, Tim. *Adapt: Why Success Always Starts with Failure*, Little, Brown (2011).

Kay, John. *Obliquity: Why Our Goals Are Best Achieved Indirectly*, Profile Books (2010).

Smith, Adam. *The Wealth of Nations*, Penguin Classics; new edition (2003).

Wolmar, Christian. *Down the Tube: The Battle for London's Underground*, Aurum Press (2002).

About the author

Rob Worth is a service design consultant specialising in helping public sector bodies such as local authorities, the NHS and government agencies to drastically improve their service and massively cut their costs.

After an MMath (Hons) in Mathematics, Rob honed his skills in the City at Chase Manhattan and JPMorgan before starting Worth Solutions Limited in 2003. He has since worked in many public and private sector organisations before deciding to put something back into society by concentrating on working with the public sector.

In addition to consulting, Rob is a writer and a speaker who believes that getting the best from any system is easier than you think if you know the right thing to look at. He is outspoken on many topics including management, systems thinking, organisational improvement, learning and excellence in public services.

Rob is based in London and can be contacted at
rob.worth@worthsolutions.com

Acknowledgements

The ideas in this book build on the work of others. It is because of the work that goes before that we don't have to start from scratch. It is to W. Edwards Deming, Taiichi Ohno, Jim Womack, Daniel Jones, Russell Ackoff, Alfie Kohn, Daniel Pink and John Seddon that I owe the deepest debt. It would benefit the reader greatly to explore their works, some of which are listed in the bibliography.

I would like to thank Isabella for being so patient and my parents for all their support over the years. Thank you too to all my friends who offered their proof reading help: Lewis, Cath, Caroline and Tanya. A big thank you to Mindy Gibbins-Klein – The Book Midwife, whose belief, patience and amazing method for structuring a book meant that I got it done in about half the time I expected. Thanks also to all my friends at the Alliance of Deming Consultants and the Transformation Forum who ensure that I keep learning every year. A big shout to the NABO folks and especially Jonathan Jay, without whom I probably wouldn't have ever sat down to write this book.